BEST PRACTICES IN SYSTEMIC STEM MENTORING

AN OFFICIAL PUBLICATION OF THE
LOUIS STOKES LOUISIANA ALLIANCE FOR MINORITY
PARTICIPATION (LS-LAMP)

ISBN: 978-0-9704609-6-7

CONTENTS

A Basis and a Guide for Best Practices in Systemic Mentoring for Broadening Participation in Science, Technology, Engineering, and Mathematics

Diola Bagayoko, PH.D., Luria Young, PH.D., and Ella Kelley, PH.D.

THE BIG PICTURE

In the following pages, we provide a summary overview of key concepts, research findings and related tautologies[1-11] on which rests the Ten-Strand Systemic Mentoring Model of the Timbuktu Academy (http://www.subr.edu/TimbuktuAcademy) and of the Louis Stokes Louisiana Alliance for Minority Participation (www.subr.edu/lslamp).

One of the most stable laws of cognitive science, the Power Law of Human Performance, and its extension, the Law of Human Performance, play a central role in the scaffolding of this model. They demystify once and for all the cumulative and integrative process of knowledge and skills acquisition and the attendant honing of thinking and reasoning capabilities. In doing so, *they underscore the ubiquitous role of appropriate exposure, efforts, and practice, from Pre-K to graduate school and beyond.* The hierarchical structure of knowledge and of some skills underscores the necessity for the proper sequencing of courses, particularly in science, technology, engineering and mathematics (STEM) disciplines.

Some comprehensive student retention[1-9] and longitudinal [10-11] studies shed further light on the crucial importance of properly sequenced learning and practice for educational success. They established [10-11] that the scope and rigor of precollege preparation, with special emphasis on mathematics, constitutes the single, greatest factor in ensuring on-time college graduation. It is not an accident that mathematics stands out in this scenario—it is the discipline with the most rigid, hierarchical, internal structure. As such, gaps in the basic mathematics background are often great obstacles—irrespective of the perceived intellectual abilities of a student. Unfortunately, most students do not know the fact that their difficulties have little to do with a lack of intelligence, rather the inadequacy of pertinent background knowledge and skills. Student retention models delve into the details of factors that govern the optimal retention and progression in and graduation from college, in general, and with a STEM degree, in particular. They serve as a basis for and a guide to systemic mentoring activities congruent with best practices.

The history of human civilization and observations of the animal kingdom show the ubiquity of the systemic preparation of youth, through training and practice, for vital tasks germane to successful adulthood. The division of labor and the intensive apprenticeship and focused practice that this preparation entails explain the emergence of expertise and proficiency that were and remain out of reach for the "unsupported, untrained, and non-specialized ones," irrespective of their genes or perceived intellect! This tautology holds true not only for humans, but also for animals that execute complex tasks (i.e., hunting) for a living. *Extraordinary proficiency or capability (i.e., prowess or genius) in architecture, mathematics, the arts, and science, for instance, was begotten through the millennia when pharaohs, emperors, kings, and other wealthy ones afforded to a select few the means and the needed time for the sustained, reflective, increasingly sophisticated practice that begets expertise in carrying out complex tasks.*

The intuitively obvious need for practice in knowledge and skills acquisition, as apparent in the above paragraph, is quantified by the Power Law of Human Performance that is applicable to the execution of simple tasks [7]. Its extension, the Law of Human Performance [7], applies to complex tasks of all kinds, including learning and doing research in STEM fields. The Law of Human Performance or of Practice [7] states the following: *Irrespective of gender, ethnicity, socioeconomic status, or other factors, the proficiency, mastery, and expertise of an individual, who is not suffering from severe physiological or mental impairments, in performing a physical (athletic), artistic (aesthetic), or intellectual (cognitive) task increase with the number of times the individual practices that task.* Academic achievement gaps, from Pre-K to graduate school and beyond, can be thoroughly and causally explained by these scientific laws which apply whether someone likes it or not. The scope and rigor of pre-college preparation, for instance, can be translated into amounts of time spent on pertinent learning tasks at the various grade levels. While adequately sequenced practice begets proficiency, the lack of it leads to deficiencies and related consequences. *Inadequacies in the above amounts of time or in the scope and rigor of the applicable subject content of courses are the ones that directly cause academic achievement gaps.*

The point above merits further elaboration, given that some books still attempt to make us believe that some innate abilities (i.e., immutable intellectual quotient-IQ) explain differences in standardized test scores of various groups of students. Bagayoko[12] recently addressed this issue by recalling the trivial way in which course-taking practices of African American, Caucasian, and Asian American students in the US, particularly in middle and high school, straightforwardly lead to their respective, average scores on the American College Test (ACT) and similar standardized tests. Differences between these average scores (i.e., achievement gaps) are far from being due to some IQ differences, as pseudo-scientifically suggested in a book in 1994. The reader is urged to consult Reference 12, freely available on the Web, to see how course-taking patterns (i.e., exposure and practice) of these three groups of students and the subject content of the ACT unambiguously explain these achievement gaps. While the IQ was basically credited for the low performance of African-American students (who did not take the needed courses), it was not for Asian Americans who outperformed whites in mathematics, due to the fact that they generally took more rigorous mathematics courses (up to pre-calculus and calculus) on average! Stephen Jay Gould's "Mismeasure of Man," first published in 1981 [13], should have totally precluded such a simplistic and utterly erroneous crediting of the IQ of some groups by a book.

The preceding points and several that follow underscore the critical need to be guided by rigorous, scientific reality. We hope that it is clear to everyone that **false IQ explanations of achievement gaps have catastrophic implications:** parents, teachers, professors and school or college administrators can blame the IQ (of students) for their failure to provide the adequate (in scope and rigor) opportunities to learn or to conduct research; similarly, funding sources can justify their divestment in human resources development, including pre-college and college education, on the account of IQ's thought to be immutable and deterministic! As for the students for whom sociocultural conditioning succeed in making them believe that they "are not smart" or "cannot do mathematics or physics"—contrary to what science says in the Power Law and the Law of Human Performance—a book may not suffice to account for all the ills exuding from this belief that is patently false. These students consequent belief in the futility of efforts and practice in learning and research, absolutely necessary for begetting proficiency and expertise, may be one of the most damning of these ills.

The Power Law and the Law of Human Performance, the clear exposé in the "Mismeasure of Man," and the recently established neural, neuronal, and brain plasticity make one thing clear: From early childhood to the doctorate degree, what society offers in a variety of ways is what mostly determines the highest level of degree attainment a person can reach by adequately applying herself or himself.

Generalities on Student Retention and Progression:

The Key Objective of Mentoring

At the college level, the term "student retention"[1-9] is understood to mean the continued and successful matriculation of a given student in a particular college curriculum. Student attrition, i.e., drop out, is naturally the opposite of student retention. A variant of retention consists of continued, successful college matriculation, but in a curriculum different from the initial one, i.e., switching. Switching out of STEM disciplines is particularly common[8]; after accounting for the pre-college preparation, it indicates a need for proactive instructional, advisement, and support activities in STEM disciplines.

Student retention and progression in the US are measured with the retention rates and graduation rates of cohorts of college students. One of the most comprehensive and authoritative source for accurate data on student retention, progression, and graduation is the National Education Longitudinal Study (NELS). In particular, high school graduates of 1982 [10] and those of 1992[11] who enrolled in college were followed for a 10-year period. The central findings of these longitudinal studies[10-11] follows.

"However complex students' attendance patterns, the principle story line leading to degrees, is that of content." Content here refers to that of the high school courses taken and also that of college courses. "The academic intensity of the student's high school curriculum still counts more than anything else in pre-collegiate history in providing momentum toward completing a *bachelor's degree.*" Adelman[11] underscored further the above finding by noting for the students who have had the needed minimum content in high school, 95% earned a bachelor's degree and 41% earned master's, first professional, or doctoral degrees by 2000.

These numbers explain the reasons A. Austin, of the Higher Education Research Institute, at the University of California at Los Angeles, contended that retention data are misleading student consumers, unwittingly or by design. Indeed, he noted that nationwide 80% of the best prepared students entering college graduate in 4 years while only 10% of the least prepared students do so. In 1994, Bagayoko and Kelley[7] introduced the Academic Preparedness Index (API) as a measure of pre-college preparation. They argued that this index should always be keyed to retention data. Failure to do so leads to confounding situations (i.e., where highly selective institutions will get student retention credits they have not "totally" earned while many other institutions will be denied retention credits they have "mostly" earned). The API is an average of appropriately scaled grade point averages and standardized test scores (i.e., American College Test or Scholastic Achievement Test).

All courses are not equal or equivalent. According to the 2006 studies of Adelman [11], the actuality of college retention indicates that the discipline where the greatest difference exists between students who earned a bachelor's degree and those who did not is mathematics: 70.5% of those who graduated completed the lower-division mathematics courses pertaining to their major (whatever that major may be) and only 37% of those who did not earn a bachelor's degree completed the lower-level mathematics courses. On page 31 of Reference 11, a table starkly tells the story: 82.1 – 83.3, 74.6 - 75.9, 7.0 – 13.4, and 3.9 – 5.4% of students who completed calculus, pre-calculus, geometry, and algebra I, respectively, earned a bachelor's degree! The first and second percentages separated by a dash, for a given level of mathematics course taking, are from the first [10] and second [11] longitudinal studies, respectively.

Adelman[11] recommends the following: "These gaps in curricular participation argue for academic administrators to identify their key gateway courses and <u>regularly monitor</u> participation." To avoid any misinterpretation of this recommendation, we recall the emphasis on content as the key story. Hence, this monitoring should never be a matter of counting the number of students who passed or failed; it must also ascertain that the students actually acquired foundational knowledge-skill contents (in scope and rigor) to pass said courses—as this foundation is critical for success in subsequent courses.

Clearly, while there are other factors that affect student retention, understanding the dominant nature of precollege preparation is of the utmost importance. Without any particular efforts on the part of institutions, retention rates for the best prepared students are much higher than those of the least prepared students. These rates include those of retention from freshman to sophomore, sophomore to junior, and junior to senior years. The 4-, 5-, and 6-year graduation rates naturally depend directly on these retention rates. **The senior bulge**, i.e., the relatively large number of seniors due to many seniors not meeting graduation requirements, naturally reduces the 4-year graduation rate. We have seen several indications that the senior bulge can generally be traced to improper sequencing of required courses. Self-advisement by students and advisement outside the major department are believed to contribute significantly to this problem.

According to Adelman [11], another factor that affects the attainment of a bachelor's degree in a modest manner is the **socioeconomic one**. Additionally, enrolling in college immediately after completing high school was shown to be correlated very strongly with earning a bachelor's degree. This factor was referred to as timing. *It should be noted here that Adelman [11] found that **gender** and **ethnicity** were never significant in the logistic narrative (i.e., no statistically significant impact could be seen for gender and ethnicity).*

Key Variable in Student Retention: A Basis for and a Guide to Effective, Systemic Mentoring

Reference 7 provides detailed discussions of the various student retention and attrition models. The reader is urged to consult this paper for an in-depth review of the prevailing theories. While some of the models are qualitative, the longitudinal-process models of Tinto[1], Beans [2], and Cabrera [3] constitute a platform for building a comprehensive student retention model with enhanced predictive capability and policy-relevance as argued by Bagayoko and Kelley [7]. Instead of repeating here the scholarly themes and issues, we focus on the summary of the findings from these models taken together. As such, this summary should therefore lead straightforwardly to concrete steps individuals, departments, and institutions can take to enhance student retention measurably. The key findings (summative variables) from the retention models follow.

Academic integration is a summative variable embodying the proper engagement of the cognitive domain of a given student. Clearly, a favorable value of this variable in college will be significantly influenced by the pre-college preparation of a student as found by Adelman [10-11]. Academic integration significantly contributes to retention and degree attainment. It is critical to note that this variable entails not only the courses taken and the sequence in which they were taken, but

13

also the degree to which a student mastered the content of said courses. Inadequacies in the scope and depth of key foundation courses (in mathematics, physics, chemistry, biology, English, etc.) lead to serious difficulties in upper level courses and to switching of majors. This variable is not just measured with the grade point average, it also includes the actual knowledge-skill contents mastered by students who passed courses, participated in research (on campus or at summer internship sites), and participated in ancillary learning activities (seminars, conferences, and others that engage cognitive and non-cognitive attributes relevant to a future profession).

Social integration is another summative variable that embodies the engagement of the affective domain of the students in a given college environment. This variable entails the goodness of the fit of a given student in the physical, social, and cultural environments of a college or university. A glance at the Maslow's need hierarchy should help a reader grasp the meaning of this variable. In plain language, as per Reference 1, *"food, housing, safety and security, social needs, and aspirations of self-actualization are critical factors in the dynamics of student retention."*

The social needs include a variety of recreational, cultural, sport, and organizational activities. Organizations in this context include societies and clubs in various disciplines, fraternities, sororities, sport teams, study groups, etc. Social integration is partly having *"a sense of belonging"* that enables the optimal functioning of the concerned student in the campus environment. Every institution should study the social integration difficulties that can be faced by "online" and "commuter" students, as well as the ones attending mostly evening or night classes. Deliberate efforts to organize gathering several times in a semester have worked for some colleges. Social integration as noted above, with positive effects on student retention and graduation, is to be distinguished from social submission, a dysfunctional situation where the goals and objectives for college attendance are lost or ignored. Proper communication and positive actions of the institution and of its personnel help to avoid undesirable consequences of mismatches between a student's assumptions, expectations, and goals and those of the institution. *Systemic mentoring is a tool that promotes and supports social integration by design!*

Students' financial status is critical in ensuring academic integration and social integration. By significantly determining the "available time" for classes, learning and research activities, this variable is at the ground level in any taxonomy of the four constructs or summative variables consisting of "financial status," "academic integration," "social integration," and "professional integration." While most institutions do not have the means to meet the financial needs of all students, federal student financial aid (including grants and loans), university wide scholarships, department or college level scholarships, along with federally and state funded supports, like the Louisiana Tuition Opportunity for Students (TOPS), are significant sources of financial support for students. *We should hasten to state here that some students may work inordinate numbers of hours per week (i.e., more than 20 hours) to meet "wants" that are sometimes confused with needs.* Additionally, meeting financial needs does not necessarily lead to full-time studying and research as it should; *well-informed institutions immerse students in a systemic mentoring environment that verifiably ensures that adequate time is devoted to class attendance, studying, homework* *completion, reviews, and learning and research projects* as opposed to assuming that to be the case.

The functionality of the Student Financial Aid Office and the degree to which departments and colleges seek student support funds from external sources will have a direct bearing on this variable. **A significant contribution of the Louis Stokes Alliances for Minority Participation programs (including Louisiana) consists of the funding provided to undergraduate STEM majors.** The financial support for the scholars is not just from the National Science Foundation, but also from a diversified funding base successfully sought by the campus mentoring infrastructure of LS-LAMP. This diverse funding base, including TOPS for the Louisiana residents who qualify for it, promotes sustainability and benefits more STEM students.

The fourth variable is professional integration. The Timbuktu Academy and LS-LAMP were among the very first, to our knowledge, to formally identify this crucial variable whose importance can be grasped by reflecting on actual practices in STEM research in private or public organizations. An understanding of the Law of Human Performance leads to the conclusion that the complex tasks to be performed in research, design, fabrication, and attendant professional cultures are learned through practice. Early research participation not only serves to apply the contents of various courses, but also to gain access to equipment and tools, not available in most college laboratories, and to experts and peers while learning a host of non-cognitive skills germane to success in a career. Professional integration therefore entails partaking in most aspects of research: literature review, problem delineation, design and execution of an experiment or the development of a theory, attendance of research group meetings, analysis of results, writing reports and papers, making presentations (at seminars and conferences), writing proposals, etc. Networking at conferences serves to build collaborations that are pivotal in tackling large scope projects or grand challenges. LS-LAMP Scholars are professionally integrated into their respective STEM disciplines partly through partaking in extensive summer research opportunities across the country. *As per the Law of Human Performance, teamwork and other facets of research are best learned through practicing them.*

Elements of the Best Practices of LS-LAMP

From the preceding sections, it clearly appears that we believe in *utilizing established facts and research findings* as bases and guides for the design and implementation of a host of activities aimed at promoting student retention in college, in general, and broadening the participation of minorities in STEM, in particular. *This scientific approach continues to take new discoveries into account.*

A second feature of the best practices of LS-LAMP *consists of the continual efforts to acquire support and funding from di-versified sources.* Even though NSF and the Louisiana Board of Regents provide the base funding for the successful operations of LS-LAMP, sustainability considerations and the need to reach as many STEM students as possible dictate this approach. One component of these efforts is the extensive leveraging of institutional resources whenever possible.

In order to ensure the academic success of LS-LAMP scholars, we developed a Strategic Implementation Plan which is a de- tailed road map for the fail-safe execution of the *Ten-Strand Systemic Mentoring Model* of the Timbuktu Academy and of LS-LAMP. To avoid redundancy, we urge the reader to consult the description of the model that follows in this book. We just note here that a mindful heeding of the Law of Human Performance pervades the model. The ten overlapping strands are:

- financial support,
- scientific advisement,
- tutoring,
- communication skill enhancement,
- generic research activities,
- the execution of specific research project,
- the deliberate immersion in a professional culture,
- continued training on tools of the trade (computers, sophisticated equipment, etc.),
- monitoring, and
- guidance to graduate school or to the job market.

Together, they ensure (a) adequate financial support to enable (b) academic integration and (c) social integration activities while comprehensively tending to the acquisition of non-cognitive skills germane to (d) success in graduate school, research careers, any profession, and in other dimensions of life.

A fourth best practice recognizes the necessary comprehensiveness of systemic mentoring. As such, it has to be woven into the core functions of the organization, i.e., teaching, research, and service activities in departments, colleges, and institutions. *This weaving requires taking systemic mentoring into account in budgeting (funding) and in evaluation!* "We do what is checked, valued, and rewarded!"

As per the ten-strands model in the next chapter, *systemic mentoring naturally integrates teaching and superior learning* (See Strands 1-3 and 8-9), on the one hand, and *teaching and research* (See Strands 5-9), on the other. Every dream is a metaphor or a paraphrase of an exposure or experience: Research experiences demystify the process and lead to big dreams of participation and contributions in years to come.

While not explicitly noted as a strand, *the continued enhancement of teaching and research infrastructure and capabilities* is integral to systemic mentoring. Our best practices therefore require that we leverage other institutional resources, including human ones, *to ensure the competitiveness of scholars* upon their graduation. It is not an accident that Physics graduates from SUBR continue to earn Ph.D. degrees from the best institutions in the country—including Georgia Tech, University of Michigan, Rice University, University of Wisconsin–Madison, University of Florida- Gainesville, Louisiana State University, University of Chicago, California Institute of Technology, Florida A&M University, MIT, Cornell, and Harvard, just to name a few. While the numbers in question are small, it is a monumental accomplishment for alumni of the Department of Physics to account for 10% of all African Americans who earned the Ph.D. in physics and directly related fields, in the United States of America, over a 14-year span (1995-2009).

Another crucial best practice of LS-LAMP resides in the *pre-college outreach of the partner campuses*, even though such activities are not supported with LS-LAMP funding from NSF. The pivotal importance of this activity is underscored by Bagayoko [12]. Indeed, as per the contents of Sections I-III above, not only is a good pre-college preparation crucial for optimal progression in and graduation from college, but also the lack of it is believed to prevent hundreds of thousands of students either from enrolling in college or from attempting STEM curriculum. This situation explains our call, during the Joint Annual Meeting of 2012, for a particular attention to "STEM the Tide" [14], a book with the distinction of grasping STEM education issues in their scope and depth, from precollege levels to college and beyond.

References and Notes

[1] Tinto, V. (1975). "Dropouts from Higher Education: A Theoretical Synthesis on Recent Research." Review of Educational Research, Vol. 45, No. 1, 89-125. The paper described the Student Integration Model (SIM) of Tinto. It is the first of the quantitative process-model and greatly influenced the ones that followed it.

[2] Bean, J. P. (1982). "Conceptual Model of Student Attrition: How Theory can Help the Institutional Researcher." Studying Student Attrition, Edited by E. T. Pascarella. San Francisco: Jossey-Bass, 17-33. The Student Attrition Model (SAM) is described in this article.

[3] Cabrera, A. F., M. B. Castaneda, A. Nora, and D. Hengstler (1992). "The Convergence between Two Theories of College Persistence." Journal of Higher Education, 63, No. 2, 144-163. This work marks the emergence of a Comprehensive Retention Model (CRM), one that incorporates the first of the two variables recommended by Bagayoko and Kelley [i.e., student financial status and time of learning tasks (TLT).]

[4] Kember, D. (1989). "A Longitudinal-Process Model of Drop-outs from Distance Education." Journal of Higher Education, Vol. 60, No. 3, 278-301. In this age of increasing distance delivery of instruction and of mentoring, this paper is quite relevant.

[5] Thompson, C. E. and R. Bruce Fretz (1991). "Predicting the Adjusting of Black Students at Predominantly White Institutions." Journal of Higher Education, Vol. 62.No. 4, 437-450.

[6] Alexander, Austin, Director, Higher Education Research Institute (HERI), University of California at Los Angeles (UCLA). Please see his articles in the Chronicle of Higher Education and several reports - many of which are annual.

[7] Bagayoko, D. and Ella L. Kelley (Fall 1994). Education, Vol. 115, No. 1, pp. 31-39. "The Dynamics of Student Retention, a Review and a Prescription." This publication explains the process of creating educational value-added, from Kindergarten through graduate school and beyond, using

the power law and the compound or Integrated Law of Human Performance (CLP or ILP). For the single task related power law of performance, please also see Newel, A. and P. S. Rosenbloom (1981). "Mechanisms of Skill Acquisition," Edited by Anderson, J. R. Hillsdale, N. J.: Erlbaum.

[8] Seymour, Elaine and Nancy M. Hewitt (1997). "Talking about Leaving: Why Undergraduates Leave the Sciences," Westview Press, Boulder, Colorado.

[9] Nora, A. (1990). "Campus-based Aid Programs as Determinants of Retention among Hispanic Community College Students." Journal of Higher Education, 61, No. 3. The title of this paper is self-explanatory.

[10] Adelman, Clifford (1999). "Answers in the Tool Box: Academic Intensity, Attendance Patterns, and Bachelor's Degree Attainment." Washington, DC: US Department of Education.

[11] Adelman, Clifford (2006). "The Toolbox Revisited: Paths to Degree Completion from High School Through College." Washington, DC: US Department of Education.

[12] Bagayoko, Diola (Fall 2013). "The Law of Human Performance and Broadening Participation in STEM," American Physical Society's CSWP and COM Gazette, Vol. 32, No. 2.

[13] Stephen Jay Gould (1981 and 1996). "The Mismeasure of Man," W. W. Norton & Company, New York, New York.

[14] Drew, David E. (2011), "STEM the Tide," Reforming Science, Technology, Engineering, and Mathematics Education in America. Johns Hopkins University Press, Baltimore, Maryland.

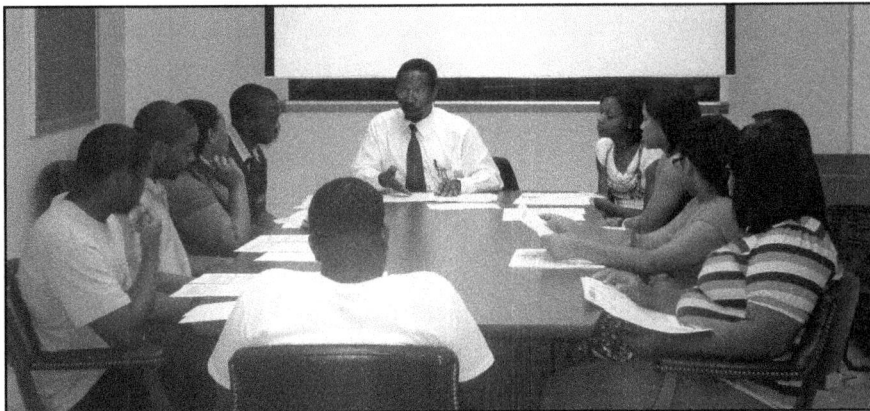

THE TEN-STRAND SYSTEMIC MENTORING MODEL

Diola Bagayoko, PH.D .

Systemic mentoring entails a weaving of the following overlapping strands. The implementation of this model and the related results earned the Timbuktu Academy Director and the Academy the 1996 and 2002 US Presidential Awards for Excellence in Science, Mathematics, and Engineering Mentoring (US-PAESMEM), respectively.

Financial Support

Financial support is provided to the scholars from a variety of sources: guidance, monitoring, and other components of the systemic mentoring guarantee the use of the resulting "time dividend" for studies, research, and related enrichment activities on a full-time basis. Continued support from LS-LAMP Phase II, for a scholar, requires full-time "studying and research" during the academic year. The diversified funding base for the scholars includes the Tuition Opportunity Program for Students (TOPS), for Louisiana residents, the Federal Student Financial Aid, and limited support from LS-LAMP and other scholarship and fellowship sources including unit and institutional funds.

Comprehensive, Scientific Advisement

The proper sequencing of courses is treated with the utmost care. Indeed, the internal rigidity (or taxonomic structure) of science, technology, engineering, and mathematics disciplines requires this approach. Empowering the learner is a central aim of mentoring. This empowerment includes grasping the Power Law of Human Performance and its extension, the Law of Human Performance (LHP), and knowing a few time-tested quotes like the Jaime Escalante Equation, its corollary, and others. The Uri Treisman discovery in Calculus, at Berkeley, is an indirect illustration of the above referenced laws that help greatly in not confusing a lack of background with a lack of intellect.

Tutoring

Tutoring by faculty members and by peers is made available to the students or scholars who need it. (In fact, regular tutoring areas are often taken over by self-organized study groups.) Tutoring is for promoting excellence, not for remediation. It is to address holes in a background and to reinforce known essentials. The need for it is not a sign of any lack of intrinsic smartness—so states the law of human performance, but rather a wise recognition of the internal rigidity of STEM fields. Incidentally, tutoring by advanced scholars also promotes their communication skills and their sense of self-worth while they review materials (so says the LHP).

Communication Skill Enhancement

A host of listening, speaking, reading, writing and related activities are aimed at developing the mastery of the applicable language (English), a vehicle of thought. This activity entails vigorous exposure to technical communication as provided for in "Writing for Success" (1998, McGraw-Hill Companies, pp. 135-176 and pp. 212-215), beyond regular English course work.

Generic Research Activities

Rigorous literature searches are conducted by the scholars on several subjects. They master sophisticated search algorithms, electronic searches, and related iterations. The scientific literature is an unlimited source of research questions. Refereed literature is the standard for STEM disciplines. Discussions of the fine structures of the scientific method, critical thinking, and creative thinking are part of this discourse.

Specific Research Project Execution

Faculty members and researchers at federal and industrial laboratories serve as research supervisors and mentors to LS-LAMP scholars. According to the law of human performance, research experiences prepare undergraduate scholars for graduate studies and for productive research careers. Seeking summer research opportunities online, at conferences, and through visits to various laboratories and agencies is one requirement for a systemic mentoring program. Assisting scholars to apply vigorously and professionally for these opportunities and maintaining adequate files on each scholar (partly for the purpose of writing substantial recommendations as opposed to general and vague ones) are some tasks for mentors to accomplish. For example, on average, 30 – 50 SUBR LS-LAMP Scholars conduct research, off-campus, during the summer. More than forty LS-LAMP scholars from across the state conduct summer research at LSU and at Tulane. Research and design infrastructure enhancement are for expanding on-campus opportunities for scholars.

Development of a Professional Culture

Every scholar is exposed to discussions that explore the dimensions of ethics in science. Immersion in a professional culture demands regular reading of technical journals and appropriate magazines of professional societies, conference attendance, and collaborations with others. Current awareness needs no explanation in an era of information explosion. Professional practices and standards are set and seen in publications, regular seminars, and at conferences. As for the need for and value of collaborations, we simply assert that no single individual has built or operated a nuclear submarine, an aircraft carrier, or a space shuttle alone! The multidimensionality and complexity of some research projects require teamwork.

Development of Computer and Technological Skills

The mastery of productivity tools, including word processing, spreadsheets, databases, graphics, and other applications and experience in scientific programming (C++, FORTRAN, etc.) are needed. Advanced exposure has to include a programming language and advanced instrumentation. The need for these activities stems from evolving practices in graduate and professional schools and the global, competitive job market.

Monitoring

With monitoring, throughout the semester, potential problems are avoided before they become permanent failures. Preventive measures include concentrated efforts, extra tutoring, and the last resort, dropping a course. The former two steps are best when they are taken as early as possible. The latter step is not an available option in most institutions past a certain date after mid-term. The monitoring of research participation and performance is critical for another reason: the development or reinforcement of non-cognitive skills that undergird success (self-discipline, hard work, assiduity, working well with others, etc.). Monitoring and evaluation are part of a professional environment. Without them, who will know what a beautiful job a scholar has done?

Guidance to Graduate School and the Job Market

Guidance to graduate school begins in the freshman year (or earlier) and includes research experiences, conference attendance, GRE preparation, and opportunities for financial support for graduate studies. Placement in graduate programs follows steps similar to those for summer placement. The number and the extent of the opportunities depend on the cumulative grade point average for the B.S. degree, the courses taken, research experiences and results, and the GRE score. In addition, graduate preparation will include an understanding of the non-academic factors that are critical to success in graduate school (study habits, self-discipline, hard work, etc.). Emphasis will be placed on the establishment of a seamless transition to graduate schools or the job market. Several of the above steps and credential requirements for the guidance to graduate or professional school are applicable to the search for rewarding positions in the job market.

BEST PRACTICES IN SYSTEMIC STEM MENTORING AT DILLARD UNIVERSITY

Abdalla Darwish, Ph.D.

To increase the institution's ranking among the nation's universities, rebuild a beautiful campus, attract top faculty and recruit the best and the brightest students, Dillard University has set eleven goals as strategic pillars. Of them, six have specific aspects where the practices of systemic mentoring are being institutionalized:

- Dillard University will expand selectively into graduate studies, building on its best programs that also represent future projections of workforce needs.

- Dillard University will increase and enhance its commitment to and production of quality research.
- Dillard University will demonstrate commitment to the success of all students.
- Dillard University will develop student leadership training and enriched educational opportunities outside of the classroom to offer a balanced environment as part of the college experience.
- Dillard University will continue to attract, retain and graduate talented African-American students, while welcoming those from diverse backgrounds who can benefit from the unique experience we offer.
- Dillard University will demonstrate commitment to technology as subject matter and as a teaching tool with the underpinnings of internal systems that are efficient and reliable.

Mission of the School of STEM

The School of Science, Technology, Engineering, and Mathematics at Dillard offers a broad spectrum of courses and experiences for students. The programs are designed with careful attention to the needs of the students, the professional preparation of the faculty, and the resources and purposes of the college. The hallmark of the program has long been its commitment to providing a quality education for students in biology, chemistry, computer science, mathematics and physics.

Strategic Priorities

In order to achieve the vision and mission of DU and the School of STEM to increase the number of STEM graduates and placing them in graduate schools, all of the STEM faculty are committed to give special attention to how they can apply and implement the strategic elements and DU pillars within their classroom and throughout their course syllabus to make sure the students take a role and responsibility of their education and are involve in all activities which enforce and advance productivity and graduation. Dillard University LS-LAMP program developed more than thirty-two activities which span the year. These LS-LAMP activities, which are based on the Ten-Strand Strategic Mentoring Model, impact the lives of STEM students at Dillard University.

School of STEM Annual Conference

This scientific conference is an annual event which brings all the STEM students in the School of STEM together for a culminating end of the year showcase of the yearlong research projects. Participants formal oral presentations are judged by a panel of faculty from in- side and outside Dillard University. The annual STEM conference is now institutionalized as part of the University during the annual undergraduate research week.

Activity Goals and Objectives
- To introduce students to research methodology in a real research laboratory doing a research activity.
- To have the students accustom to scientific research methods and hands-on, minds-on training for STEM students on scientific research methodology and reporting such as scientific writing.
- To train the student to set up a poster for judging.
- To enhance the student's oral communication through learning how to use Standard English in oral presentations.

This is an open showcase for other Dillard University students to learn about the other research activities within the STEM areas which can result of exchange of ideas, produce interest in collaborations. Award all the mentors, STEM faculty, students, and the

administration for their effort in institutionalization of the LS-LAMP program. Make the administration from top-down to be involved on the process and educate them about the needs of the STEM students.

Outcomes

All level I LS-LAMP scholars and all level II scholars including all the other STEM scholars who participated in the one-day scientific conference, and competed for awards, which their presentation were judged by faculty. This conference is the showcase for STEM students to compete, and exchange research information.

All the winners were recognized with trophies, plaques, monetary awards, and certificates for completion of all program requirements. The closing ceremony is always attended by the dean of the College of Arts and Science, the provost, the president, and all other administrators. The administration's support signifies the role of the program on the lives of the STEM scholars across the school of STEM.

Course Advising

The general advising of the students occurs during the pre-registration for Fall, Spring, Summer I and Summer II. Faculty should be in their offices during the advising time. The dean of the school and every chair are responsible of monitoring the process and reporting back to the provost and vice president for academic affairs.

Activity Goals and Objectives
1. Guide the students through their course of the study
2. Deal with specific issues of retention, major changes, and three programs
3. Maintain the students on course and ensure the proper time of graduation is met
4. Audit seniors to ensure their on-time graduation and making sure they completed all graduation requirements

Outcomes
1. Retain the students in STEM majors
2. Ensure the proper classes were registered and the pre-requisites were met
3. Ensure the graduation of the students on time and after capturing any problem early on which will stop their graduation
4. Ensure the compliance with divisional and university requirements, like passing the comprehensive exam on time and completing volunteer hours
5. Ensure the adequate preparation for GRE exams and the requirements for graduate schools

Curriculum Reform

The university catalog goes under revision each year for the last five years. A review for all academic departments is underway. A reform of the core curriculum for all STEM departments' catalogs was done last year, now the University is in a process of revamping the core curriculum. In addition, a complete revamp of the entire STEM courses and class pre-requisites are underway.

Activity Goals and Objectives
1. To ensure that the curriculum aligned in such a way to enhance students' communication skills
2. To introduce STEM students to research tools, methods, and performance
3. To prepare students for graduate school. All the above will result from this activity which in turn will introduce a new concept into the classroom, in teaching strategies and technology in classroom
4. To have the core courses to match the university vision and mission
5. To revisit the engineering agreements with UNO, Georgia Tech, and Tulane University
6. To introduce scientific research methods to all STEM scholars and the model to the entire University

This will strengthen the students background in many major areas like mathematics, physics, and engineering which will build a foundation for their research as well as graduate studies. In addition, it will put our students on the graduate level and insure their success.

Outcomes
Through the University Core Curriculum Committee, the chairs of STEM departments were able to revisit all the STEM course materials and update the textbooks and the teaching methodolo-

gy in the department. We expect a strong core curriculum which will support the students learning and culture at DU.

Career Fair

The Dillard University career fair day allows the students to engage in professional discussion with upscale employee and companies. This gives the students and the interviewer a preview of one another. The students prepare their resume and dress professionally for this pre-interview day.

Activity Goals and Objectives

To help the scholars find jobs during and after the academic year as well as during the summer time. Also, it helps them for Networking, graduate opportunities, Industry. This secure either job, or graduate program for the students.

Outcomes

The career fair assisted many STEM students in applying for graduate programs and careers.

Peer Assistant Students Support

The LS-LAMP STEM students have to spend eight hours per month tutoring other students at the student support service learning center. This make them active on their field of study and improve their understanding of the materials and prepare them for the GRE exam.

Activity Goals and Objectives

To enhance the STEM majors in both STEM and non-STEM classes, to enhance their academic performance, study skills and construct group study among them. The Learning Center activity is an important element of the LS-LAMP program and the DU

support services as it partners natural science faculty with STEM students and involve them in different activities including tutoring and advising.

Outcomes

Through peer tutoring and helping one another to comprehend STEM disciplines, students gain enhancement of their overall grade point average. Often a large number of students in the same STEM classes are found at the DU-LAMP Learning Center in-groups and one-to-one tutoring secessions. This increased the capacity of the tutoring service to serve more students and to enhance the outreach of the center. The scholars get more hands-on training on the problem solving and critical thinking which are essential for all classes.

Guidance Toward Graduate Schools

Mentors and advisors gear scholars to graduate programs through preparation courses and the DU-LAMP GRE Examination. The School of STEM has established a graduate committee to support this activity.

Activity Goals and Objectives

In the junior year, the mentor takes a focused direction for gearing the scholar to graduate school. By the senior year the scholars have been introduced, groomed and inducted to the expectation of graduate studies. All STEM students entering graduate schools should take GRE preparatory courses. The scholar usually has been involved in several summer research experiences, which is used as catalysts for graduate programs. Students apply to at least five graduate programs.

Outcomes

The number of STEM scholars attending graduate programs continues to increase, and the enrollment of STEM students steady increase. Other scholars pursue careers which afford them the opportunity to work for a company which usually pays for graduate school.

Graduate Schools Preview Weekend

This is an excellent opportunity to visit graduate school and laboratories to get a first-hand look at the technology being researched and a personal introduction to graduate students. Furthering the scholars become familiar with the structure of the campus and laboratory.

Activity Goals and Objectives
1. To introduce the scholar to graduate students graduate faculty and their research
2. To secure graduate scholarship for DU-LS-LAMP students
3. To explore different possibilities of graduate program to shape up their visions and make them more focused of career planning.

Outcomes
Every year, many scholars were invited by different graduate programs and some had the opportunity to visit with more than one University. The travel and accommodation was paid by the hosting institute. Due to the paid visit, it made it accessible to many of our scholars to visit and negotiate the acceptance to graduate programs like Georgia Tech, Nebraska University, Columbia University, Cal Tech, Colorado University and MIT.

Graduate Student Tracking
To check on the status of the prior graduated STEM scholars to deduce whether they have entered into a graduate program, continued the graduate program, obtained a graduate degree or corporate business employment and keep an updated data.

Activity Goals and Objectives
To get a clearer picture of the DU-LS-LAMP mentoring component and to steer the scholar to graduate/doctorate program. Also, to measure the effectiveness' merit factor for the success of the LS-LAMP program goals.
Outcomes

The DU-LS-LAMP office is continuing the collection of accumulative comprehensive database about which is used in many different ways to show the effectiveness of the academic performance of the DU STEM-students and the LS-LAMP program. Also, updating the senior exit form provides the DU-LS—LAMP office with information to follow up of academic/employment performance of DU graduates through e-mails and telephone calls and personal visit to their campus. In addition, the Alumni association is a tool to track and capture the momentum of DU graduate beyond Dillard University.

Scientific Conference and Meetings
Activity Goals and Objectives
1. To enhance the level of research and training for the faculty and students
2. To introduce new way and ideas for relating to the research and interact with the scientific community
3. To networking the scholars with other partners in the scientific community
4. To give the students extended exposure to other scientific research and conference presentation experience
5. To have close relation with other scientists in the field and develop collaborations through research projects
6. To interest and retain talented undergraduate minority students in academic careers.
7. To enhance STEM scholars preparation for graduate study through intensive research experiences and presentations with faculty mentors.

Outcomes
The STEM scholars attended many scientific conferences, presented, competed, and—at many instances—won competi-

tions including first and second. Some of these meetings include: the Annual Biomedical Research Conference for Minority Students; Emerging Researchers National Conference; Fattah Conference; Annual Beta Kappa Chi and National Institute of science Honor Societies joint conference; Dillard University Mathematics in College Life Essay Presentations; Dillard University Math Relay; National Annual LS-LAMP/ GAELA conference at the University of Arizona; the annual National Society of Black Physicists conference; and the annual meeting of National Society of Black Engineers.

Mentoring

Mentors give guidance and instruction to students, while providing research topics and direction for individual projects. In an effort to promote research endeavors and other self-directed inquiries, mentors provided laboratory-oriented support and hands-on experiences with emphasis on strategies for increasing students' self-confidence, motivation, critical and analytical thinking skills, and creativity.

Activity Goals and Objectives
1. To increase minority students' level of interest and motivation in STEM fields
2. To increase the academic preparedness of talented students for college careers in STEM
3. To increase the number of Dillard students with leadership abilities in STEM
4. To increase the number of talented Dillard students graduating with baccalaureate degrees in STEM fields well-prepared for graduate studies

5. To increase steadily Dillard's retention of minority students in STEM disciplines

Increase in the quality of instruction, academic support services and laboratory experiences in the STEM fields are in order to increase the preparedness of students for graduate study. The goals and objectives are aimed at fostering the development and enhancement of intellectual skills, self-confidence in science and mathematics disciplines, and the mentoring of students to discover their potentials in STEM careers. All the above enable students to have hands-on training and preparation for graduate schools.

Outcomes

Faculty mentoring (which is LS-LAMP's Systemic Mentoring) began with few faculty who are committed to the mission. Over the years, the program became very popular and was used as a measure of faculty performance in the School of STEM. This year, we have all faculty in the School as team members of this program. Of course, there is no way to have all faculty cover all the students at the school, but, each faculty has three or four mentees. This is different from academic advisor. In some cases, the academic advisor is the same as the mentor and in addition to volunteer tutoring for hours weekly. This supports the STEM student retention and steers them toward graduate schools. The school of STEM continues to adopt the DU-LS-LAMP systemic mentoring outlines which was proved and tested for the last few years and found to be working with DU STEM students. This has many advantages to STEM majors as reported before:

1. Students become more academically and mentally prepared for graduate school and become more organized, focused, and dedicated to any research program.

2. Students are provided with research experiences and development of critical thinking skills which are valuable upon matriculation from undergraduate studies.
3. Monitoring is a role model type activity, which will easily spot a "Toxic prot'g's" and correct the student's line activities for more improving will be required.
4. Students learn the basic tools for research, thinking, administrating their research project, managing their time wisely, and communicating their results and findings to others

Institutionalization of the LS-LAMP Program

A central focus for LS-LAMP campus coordinators remains to ensure the institutionalization of the LS-LAMP program and most its activities after the grant's lifetime at Dillard University and the School of STEM.

Activity Goals and Objectives

1. To involve all the senior administrators in the program activities
2. To educate the administration about the needs of STEM majors
3. To gain support for different activities, which could be realized as part of the university wide performance, such as research, mentoring, scientific presentation, conference attendances, recruiting, and retention.

Outcomes

1. The University president, provost and senior officials attend and are recognized during the annual STEM science conference which is sponsored by DU LS-LAMP program

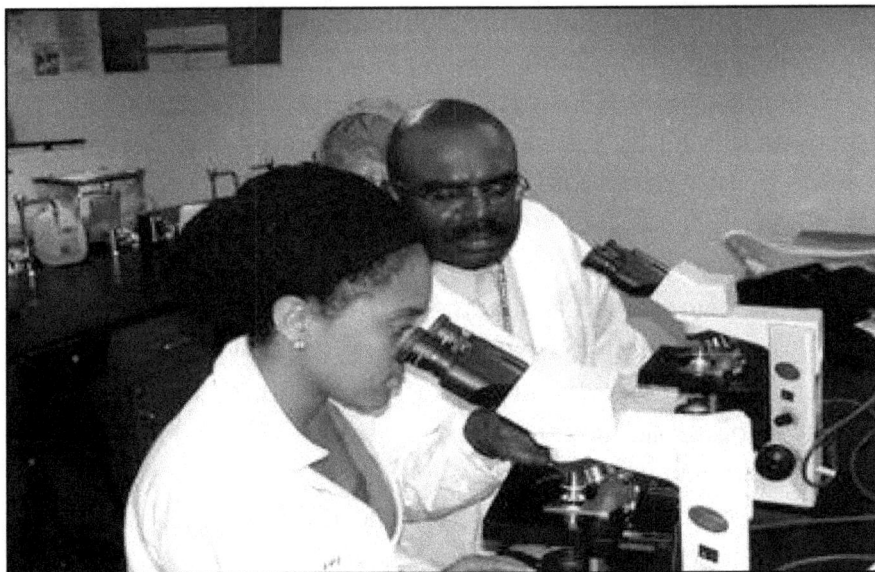

2. The senior exit form, one of the priorities of the LS-LAMP pro-gram, became part of the School of STEM graduation package.

3. The supervising of the learning center was moved from the physics department where it was initiated originally to the School of STEM as a result of institutionalizing LS-LAMP and to ensure accountability.

4. An increase in faculty writing grants due to a key concept that this is highlighted in the Faculty Handbook which im-plemented and emphasized the importance of grant writ-ing and publication when measuring merit pay, faculty tenure, and promotion. As a result more grant proposals were submitted by the DU faculty.

5. Annual science research conference held during under-graduate research week became part of the University's official event calendar.

Scientific Publications

Scientific papers are published or presented at scientific conferences to support the students in their graduate programs and help to build their resume.

Activity Goals and Objectives
1. To give students documented research opportunities for training and recognition
2. To enhance scholars' scientific writing, oral presentation, and public speaking skills through presentation during scientific conferences
3. To expose scholars to scientific publication ideology and methodology
4. To enhance student portfolios

Outcomes
Many papers with the students as co-authors have been accepted or published in scientific publications. As a result, STEM departments have been recognized for the research activities and received increased support of extramural funds from local and federal grants.

Scientific Societies
To involve the students in different scientific societies which were established by the program director like Optical Society of America, National Society of Black Engineers, American Physics Students, Society of Physics Students, the International Society of Optical engineering, and National Society of Black Physicists.

Activity Goals and Objectives

1. To encourage the student to pursue graduate studies in physics, engineering, or other STEM field through networking
2. To provide an opportunity where NSBE introduces STEM students into sciences and technologies fields, which will be available to them upon completion of a B.S. degree
3. To inform the scholar of M.S. and Ph.D. required fields and the monetary values of pursuing such degrees
4. To encourage STEM students to participate in traveling and presenting during annual meeting of these societies for learning and career planning in STEM fields
5. To train students on self-governing the Society chapters at Dillard University
6. To support students transform themselves into contributing members of the professional community and established a strong networking group
7. To give students a strong experience in Leadership, establish-ing a personal network of contacts, presenting scholarly work in professional meetings and journals, and outreach services to the campus. These skills are needed to flourish professionally the DU students.

Outcomes

Meetings under the direction of the academic advisor, are taking place monthly to plan the society's activities, trips, and fund raising. In addition, a bi-monthly the meetings are held over the internet and during the summer. The students are exposed to current research information. The students' activities and leadership is enhanced and the level of activities increased . In addition, the societies engaged them in scientific discussions around the monthly meetings where they select topic and make it as a round table discussion and invite scholars from around the city and nationally to attend. This is a culture change at Dillard University and gives a new meaning to the student university life.

Summer Internships

Summer internships help STEM students find summer enrichment Internships/fellowship programs that will allow the student to participate in research or learning activities or even co-op program which will be a summer job then a full time employment in STEM area could be secured early on.

Activity Goals and Objectives
1. To secure summer internships for STEM majors
2. To provide the STEM student with experience in research and internship
3. To actively involve the students in year-round learning process
4. To introduce the students to the real world activities, which will give them strong hands-on experience and minds-on training and the sense of accountability and responsibility
5. To enable the scholars to explore more interesting fields and discover themselves under real accountable activities
6. To support the scholars to discover their interests and plans to satisfy their goals

Outcomes

As part from the school of STEM and DU graduation requirements, each STEM student has to spend one summer internship in an organized research project at major research university or national laboratory. Many STEM students secure a summer REU position.

Summer Scholarship Assistance

Summer scholarship assistance financially supports some of the students to register for summer classes to speed up their graduation or to put them back on track for graduation.

Activity Goals and Objectives
1. To assist the STEM scholar in enhancing their academic GPA
2. To increase academic year class load for the scholar
3. To put some students on track or course sequence and have to enroll in summer classes to increase the possibilities of graduation on time
4. To increase the extra curriculum activities and to enhance some of the students' performance. This will increase the retention on the STEM fields and provide them with scientific advising

Outcomes

Many students who participated in this activity enhanced their GPA and were on track with a timely graduation. This increased the number of graduates in STEM fields.

External Funding

Faculty write grants and submit proposals to local and federal department and foundation.

Activity Goals and Objectives
1. To increase the Research opportunities and proposal writing for external funds to enhance the student opportunity of learning, research and teaching instruction, scholarship opportunities, GRE exam, and research infrastructure

2. To gear them toward graduate schools
3. To secure external funding for the further enhancement of student education and research training
4. To provide students with other avenues of internship funding

Outcomes

The faculty secured millions of dollars from different resources which enhanced the research laboratories infrastructure, students support during summer time, and in turn increased the publications. In addition, having strong fund increased the enrollment of these programs which attracts more students due to the research stipend.

Conclusion

Dillard University LS-LAMP program followed the blue print of the ten-strand systemic mentoring model. This model is a strong scientific recipe of success which fits any academic field and any academic program under any circumstances or budget issues. Dillard University has benefit for the funding of LS-LAMP and used as a seed money to build stronger academic programs and infrastructure through millions of dollars of funding which increased the retention graduation rate and placing students into graduate programs.

BEST PRACTICES IN SYSTEMIC STEM MENTORING AT GRAMBLING STATE UNIVERSITY

Olusegun Adeyemi, PH.D., Danny Hubbard, PH.D., Melvenia Martin, PH.D., and Leonard Moore Jr., PH.D.

Grambling State University, located in the city of Grambling, in Northwestern Louisiana, is a historically Black university founded in 1901. The University has been accredited by thirteen accrediting associations, including the Commission on Colleges of the Southern Association of Colleges and Schools and holds accreditations in all programs required by the Louisiana Board of Regents. Grambling State University is a member of the University of Louisiana System.

Grambling State University is a comprehensive institution offering baccalaureate, masters, and doctoral programs on its 590-acre campus. As a component of its mission, the university seeks to provide opportunities for students to develop intellectually and to acquire appropriate career skills through instruction, research, public service, and special programs. The academic program is designed to meet the needs of all students enrolled, including those who may have been adversely affected by educational, social and/or economic deprivation. Many of GSU's students are first generation college students and come from socially and economically deprived backgrounds. More than 85% of the student body receives financial aid. In 2007, the University began a gradual implementation of selective admissions requirements, as mandated by the State of Louisiana. These requirements were fully implemented by the fall of 2010.

The area of Academic and Student Affairs at Grambling State University includes three college divisions: Arts and Sciences; Business; and Educational, Professional, and Graduate Studies. The College of Arts and Sciences consists of twelve departments, including five representing STEM areas. These are biological sciences, chemistry, computer science, engineering technology, and mathematics/physics.

In 2009, Grambling State University ranked 55th among all institutions in awarding undergraduate degrees to African Americans. In 2013, the University ranked 45th among all US baccalaureate origin institutions of 2002-2011 African-American science and engineering doctorate recipients. Grambling State University has a long-standing record of participating in programs with goals and objectives that are consistent with the LS-LAMP Program. Such programs include the Maximizing Access for Research Careers (MARC), and the Center for Mathematical Achievement in Science and Technology (CMAST). Each program supports undergraduate students through scholarships, tutoring, mentoring, and undergraduate research participation.

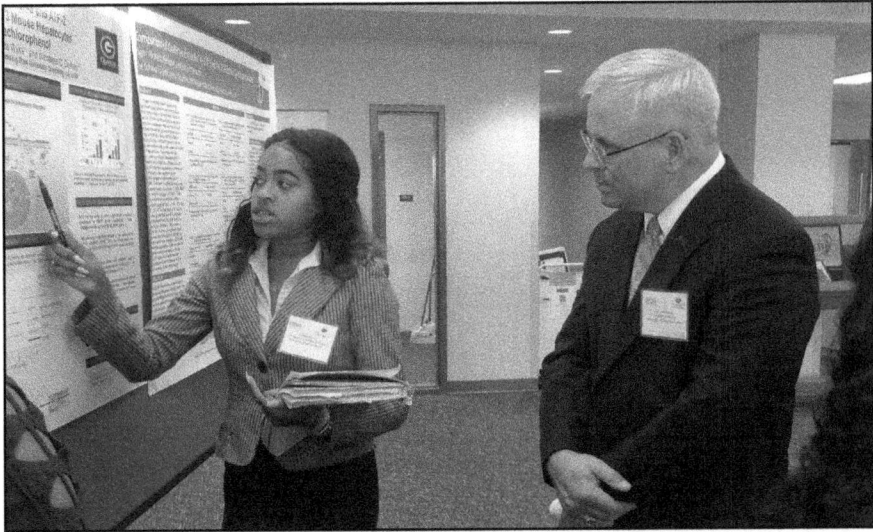

Overall Goals and Objectives

The overall objective of the LS-LAMP program at GSU is to increase the number and quality of minorities receiving baccalaureate degrees in STEM fields and to assist in increasing the number of these graduates in successful pursuit of STEM graduate degrees with emphasis on the Ph.D. Under the leadership of campus coordinators and the dean and associate dean of the College of Arts & Sciences, the LS-LAMP Program at GSU offers students the following opportunities to insure their success while attending GSU and prepare them for their future endeavors:

- Book Award
- Supplemental Peer Instruction
- Research and Conference Opportunities
- Summer Internship Opportunities
- Application Assistance
- GRE Preparation
- LS-LAMP Cadet Award

Systemic Mentoring Activities

Expansion of Financial Support to GSU Students

Many of GSU students are first-generation college students and come from socially and economically deprived backgrounds. More than 85% of these students receive financial aid in the forms of scholarships, grants and loans; many of them work in order to support their families and/or reduce their debt burden, and a size-able number of them often do not purchase required text-books.

Expanding financial support to our students has the effect of relieving them of high debt burden as well as allowing them to spend more time on their studies. The following programs repre-sent sources of financial support to STEM majors at GSU:

- LS-LAMP Book Awards. GSU STEM majors who participate in the LS-LAMP program receive book awards each se-mester. At the end of each semester students are required to return awarded books they no longer need to the pro-gram office. Returned books are then made available to other students in subsequent semesters. Students must maintain a minimum grade point average in order to contin-ue in the program.

- The Center for Mathematical Achievement in Science and Technology. The program supports STEM freshmen with scholarships and book awards. These students also are also placed in a Learning Community and a couple of common courses during the fall and spring semesters. The program is supported by a NSF HBCU-UP grant.

- The MARC Program supports junior and senior STEM ma-jors. The MARC program is a grant that supports biology, chemistry, computer science, and mathematics/physics ma-

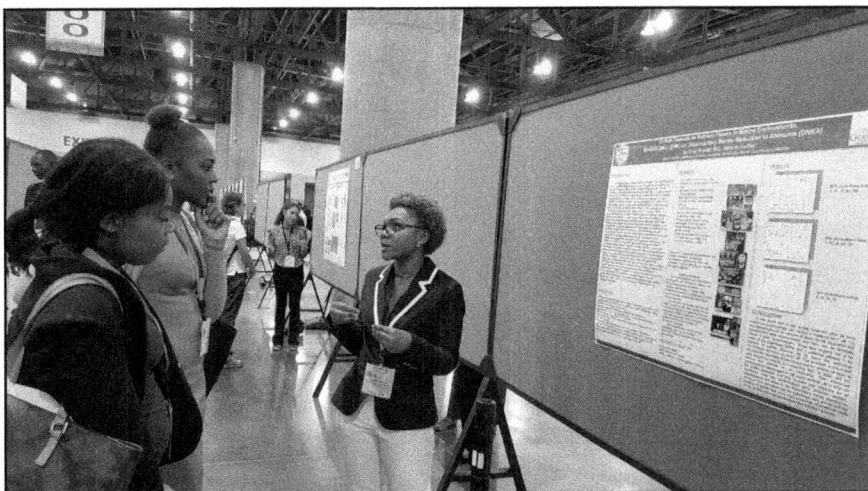

jors in their junior and senior years with full scholarships. The MARC Scholarships are funded by the National Institute of General Medical Science/National Institutes for Health (NIGMS/NIH).

- Louisiana TOPS scholarship. The Taylor Opportunity Program for Students is a program of state scholarships for Louisiana residents who attend Louisiana colleges and universities.

Communication Skill Enhancement

Each STEM degree program includes an Advanced Technical Writing course in their curriculum. Many of the courses in science and engineering technology have associated laboratory components. These components provide opportunities for students to work together collaboratively in performing required experiments, writing necessary reports and making presentations. Also, every STEM student takes discipline-specific seminar or senior (research) project courses in their majors during their junior and/or senior years. Students submit formal written reports and make presentations of their project/research work to students and faculty members. Some of the projects have resulted in journal publications and conference presentations. A writing laboratory has been dedicated to the improvement of communication skills of all GSU students. This laboratory which is located in the English department opened during the Spring 2013 semester. Students can receive help on any aspect of their writing.

Comprehensive Scientific Advisement

The objective of the activities in this area is to help students navigate their curriculum and prepare them for their intended career or graduate program.

Each STEM student is assigned a faculty advisor in their major as soon as they declare a major. A student cannot enroll in any course at GSU without an Alternate PIN which the faculty advisor provides only after the student has been duly advised. Both the student and the advisor also sign an Academic Advising Contract to document this process. On the contract, the student agrees to inform his/her advisor of subsequent changes to their schedules. Each STEM department holds regular meetings with their majors during the year. Each student is provided a copy of his/her curriculum sheet; a copy of the curriculum sheet is also kept in the student's advisement folder which is kept in the department or advisor's office.

In addition, discipline-specific seminar courses built into each STEM program provided professional advisement to students. Information on internship and graduate school opportunities are disseminated to students through the department offices and by email.

LS-LAMP supported research activities. Students are encouraged to work under the supervision of a research mentor who emphasizes importance of graduate school admission and the opportunity to receive stipends. STEM faculty members are also involved in identifying and nominating students for stipend support.

Tutoring

Grambling State University recognizes that most of our students need tutoring, some for remediation and some for excellence. University-wide tutoring services are available through the Office of Retention. The office provides supplemental instruction, peer instruction and tutoring, and early alert by working with faculty to identify and notify students who are in danger of failing their classes. Another university-wide tutoring service is provided by mathematics faculty.

Locations and schedules of tutoring services are publicized through all campus media outlets every semester. Discipline-specific tutoring services offered by faculty and student chapters of professional societies are also available to STEM majors. In addition, every faculty member is required to commit at least ten hours a week to be available in their offices to tutor and mentor students. Information on the tutorials is posted on both physical and electronic notice boards in all science and engineering technology buildings. E-mail messages are also sent to students to provide further details about tutoring sessions.

In addition, the quality enhancement plan has a focus to improve the mathematical skills of all students enrolled at Grambling State University. Faculty members and students with strong backgrounds in mathematics work with the students via the mathematics clinic to hold individual help sessions relevant to students' needs or weaknesses; they also encourage their students to attend tutoring sessions throughout the semester.

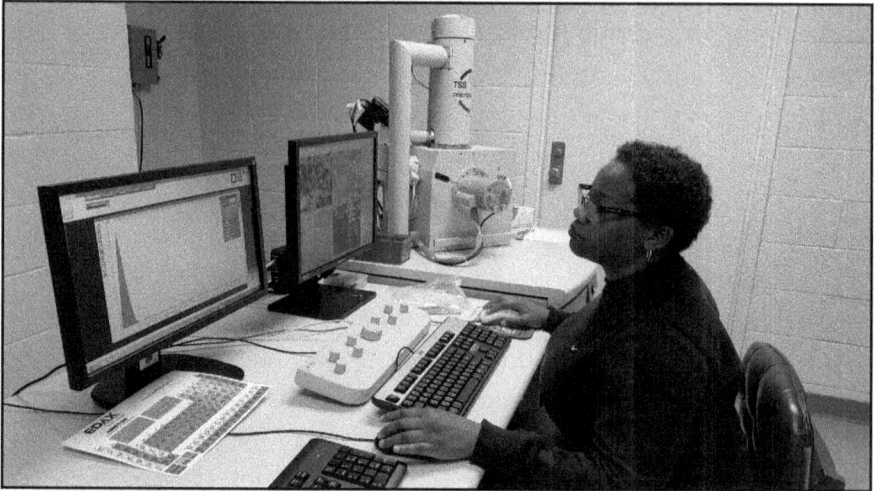

Exposure to Research and Opportunities that Build Professional Skills

In efforts to motivate students to success in STEM beginning their first year at the University, all STEM programs at GSU include some aspect of research in their courses, including introductory level courses. Process Oriented Guided Inquiry Learning and Problem-Based Learning/Project-Based Learning instructional strategies are employed in several STEM introductory level courses.

At the beginning of each summer, the CMAST program supports a number of students in a Rising Sophomore Academy. This program is designed to introduce students to research. Selected students work on various research topics under the supervision of four faculty members. Each student receives a stipend at the conclusion of the program. The MARC program includes mandatory summer research internships at university or national research laboratories for all participants. However, all eligible STEM students are encouraged to apply for summer internship opportunities.

The LS-LAMP program also supports a number of students with stipends to work with faculty on research projects during the year. Some of these activities often result in journal publications and/or presentations at conferences. In addition, senior and junior STEM majors take discipline-specific seminar and/or senior (research) project courses in their majors during the year. Guest speakers are invited to address current issues and professional standards in their fields.

Development of Computer and Technological Skills

The objective of this activity is to provide opportunities for students to become familiar with computer applications and technological tools relevant to their disciplines. GSU operates two types of computer laboratories on campus:

Open Computer Laboratories
These laboratories include:
- Writing Laboratory which is located in the English department. It is dedicated to the improvement of communication skills of all GSU students. Students can receive help on any aspect of their writing.
- Curriculum Resource and STEM Academic Success Center is available to all STEM majors. Services available include: study skills assessment and workshop; mathematics tutorials; GRE preparation resources; reference materials; etc.
- Quality Enhancement Plan, or QEP, Mathematics Clinic is equipped with a computer laboratory and workspace dedicated to providing tutorial assistance to all students in the improvement of mathematical skills and knowledge.

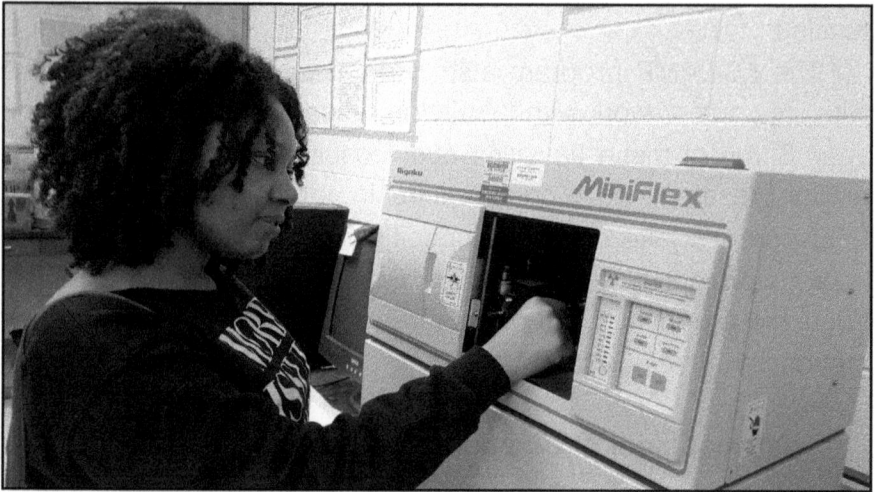

Discipline-Specific Laboratories

Each STEM discipline at GSU has dedicated laboratories, including computer laboratories where equipment and computer software unique to that discipline are made available to their students. While use of some of these laboratories is often tied to specific courses, departments such as computer science and engineering technology have open laboratories which are available for their majors to use outside of their classes. These laboratories are updated regularly to ensure that they meet the accreditation requirements.

Monitor Student Performance

The GSU Office of Retention works with faculty to identify students who are at risk of failing courses using an Early Alert System procured by the university. Appropriate intervention strategies are recommended for such students. The office also provides supplemental instruction, peer instruction and tutoring for students. Academic advisors are also involved in monitoring performance of their advisees as they interact with them throughout the year and especially following midterm examinations when students begin making plans for their next semester. The LS-LAMP program obtains information about student GPAs every semester. Students whose GPA falls below a set minimum are placed on probation or suspended from the program. Students may also forfeit their opportunity to continue to receive textbook awards. LS-LAMP participants on the Honor Roll are recognized during the University's Honors Day Convocation in March and at a special LS-LAMP ceremony at an end of April.

Preparation of Students for Graduate School

This is one of the main goals of the LS-LAMP program and as such several activities are focused on it throughout the year. The first meeting of the year, held usually in September, is utilized to emphasize the importance of these activities to the achievement of the goals of the program. Students' responsibilities in this regard and availability of campus resources are discussed at length. GRE workshops are organized by various programs during the year. These programs include MARC and RISE. The CMAST program office has also made available GRE preparation materials and practice exams for all STEM majors. The Curriculum Resource and STEM Academic Success Center laboratory is available to all STEM majors. Services available include: study skills assessment and workshop; mathematics tutorials; GRE preparation resources, etc. Several graduate school recruiters visit GSU during the year. These include the annual visit of the Big Ten Schools Recruitment Caravan, the University of Illinois at Chicago, and many universities from neighboring states.

Students also have opportunities to receive information about graduate schools at professional meetings and conferences. For example, each of the twenty students who attended the 2013 Annual NSBE convention in Indianapolis was able to speak with graduate school representatives and representatives of Fortune 500 companies during a two-day career fair. Information on internships and graduate school opportunities are made available to students through various campus media outlets, including GSU radio, electronic bulletin boards, posters, and class announcements. LS-LAMP campus coordinators email information about internships and graduate school opportunities to students as they became available throughout the year.

Conclusion

Many of GSU students are first generation college students and come from socially and economically deprived backgrounds. More than 85% of the student body receives financial aid. Access to programs such as LS-LAMP, MARC and CMAST is therefore very important, not only to their success at graduating with STEM degrees, but more so for their preparation for graduate school. The activities implemented in the LS-LAMP program are particularly helpful for students outside of the limited scopes of other programs.

Books are made available through the program often make the difference between withdrawing from a course due to a student falling too far behind, staying in class that a student knows he/she is failing in order to meet financial aid minimum credit hour requirement, and a student completing the course with a passing grade. Workshops, meetings and seminars relating to graduate school opportunities and benefits often represent the first contacts many of our students have with such subjects. Here are some GSU LS-LAMP success stories:

- Joel K. Durand, GSU LS-LAMP scholar, obtained his B. S. degree in chemistry at Grambling State University in December 2009. In February 2010, he was awarded a research assistantship at the Laboratory of Bernard Weissman, Ph.D. in the Department of Genetics & Molecular Biology, University of North Carolina, Chapel Hill, NC. He is currently a Ph.D candidate.

- Whitney I. Henry obtained her degree in biological sciences in May 2010. Harvard University awarded her a full scholarship in its Biological and Biomedical Sciences Program where she is currently pursuing a Ph.D. She completed undergraduate research at Grambling State University.

- Melvenia Martin, Ph.D., is a 1997 graduate of the Biological Science Program at Grambling State University. She entered a graduate program in the Cellular & Molecular Biology Department at Tulane University. In 2000, she completed the requirements for the master of science degree in toxicology and in 2006, she was awarded a doctorate in molecular and cellular biology from Brown University. She worked as a post-doctoral fellow at the National Institute of Health's National Cancer Institute. She was one of our early LS-LAMP participants while at GSU.

- Zenia Norman graduated from GSU in May 2012 with double majors in drafting and design engineering technology and electronics engineering technology. She is pursuing a Ph.D. in biomedical engineering at the University of Missouri, Columbia.

- In 2004, Ernest Ricks graduated cum laude with a bachelor's degree in biology. He was admitted to the Ph.D. program at Morehouse School of Medicine and later joined the Cardiovascular Research Institute at Morehouse and received a National Institute of Health Fellowship in 2006. During the fall of 2008, Ricks joined the laboratory of Methods Bacanamwo, Ph.D., and started a project centered on the role of epigenetics in vascular cell fate. Research findings from this project could be useful in the prevention of atherosclerosis, hypertension, and congestive heart failure. Ricks earned a Ph.D. in biomedical sciences from Morehouse School of Medicine in 2011.

References

"Top 100 Degree Producer 2009" Diverse Issues in Higher Education.

"Baccalaureate Origins of US-Trained S&E Doctorate Recipients," M' K. Fiegener and Steven L. Proudfoot. National Center for science and engineering Statistics, NSF 13-323. April 2013.

Bunch, G. (2009). "Going up there": Challenges and opportunities for language minority students during a mainstream classroom speech event. *Linguistics and Education: An International Research Journal*, 20 (2), 81–108.

Committee on science, engineering, and Public Policy. (2007). Rising above the gathering storm: Energizing and employing America for a brighter economic future. Retrieved February 25, 2008, from National Academies Press website, http://www.nap.edu/cata- log/11463.html

Espinosa, L. (2009). Pipelines and pathways: Women of color in STEM majors and the experiences that shape their persistence. Unpublished doctoral dissertation.

Higher Education Research Institute.(2010). Degrees of success: Bachelor's degree completion rates among initial STEM majors. Retrieved on March 1, 2010,from http://www.heri.ucla.edu/nih/ HERI_Research-Brief_OL_2010_STEM.pdf

Huang, G., Taddese, N., & Walter, E. (2000). Entry and persistence of women and minorities in college science and engineering education (No. NCES 2000601). Washington, D.C.: National Center for Educa- tion Statistics.

Hunter, A. B., Laursen, S. L., & Seymour, E. (2006). Becoming a scientist: The role of undergraduate research in students' cognitive, personal, and professional development. Science Education, 91(1), 36–74

Kaltenbaugh, L. S., St. John, E. P., and Starkey, J. B. "What Difference Does Tuition Make? An Analysis of Ethnic Differences in Persistence." Journal of Student Financial Aid, 1999, 29(2), 21–31.

Ladson-Billings, G. (1995). Toward a theory of culturally relevant pedagogy. American Educational Research Journal, 32 (3), 465– 491.

Laursen, S., Seymour, E., Hunter, A. B., Thiry, H., & Melton, G. (2010). Undergraduate research in the sciences: Engaging students in real science. San Francisco: Jossey-Bass.

Seymour, E., Hunter, A.-B., Laursen, S., & Deantoni, T. (2004). Es- tablishing the benefits of research experiences for undergraduates in the sciences: First findings from a three-year study. Science Edu- cation, 88(4), 493–534.

Peng, P. and S. Hill, Characteristics and educational experiences of high-achieving minority students in science and mathematics, Journal of Women and Minorities in science and engineering, 1 (2), 137-152 (1994).

Jacobi, M., Mentoring and Undergraduate Academic success: A literature review, Review of Educational Research, 61(4), 505-32 (1991).

Hurte, V.J. Mentoring: the forgotten retention tool, Black Issues in Higher Education 19 (18) 49 (2002).

Stromei, L.K., Increasing retention and success through mentoring,, New Direction for Community Colleges, no 112,San Francisco. Jossey-Bass. (2000)

Blackwell, J. Mentoring: An action strategy for increasing minority faculty, Academe 75, 8-14 (1989).

Brown II, M. Christopher and Guy L. Davis and Shederick A. McClen- don, Mentoring Graduate Students of Color: Myths, Models, and Modes, Peabody Journal of Education, 74(2), 105-118 (1999).

Boyer, E. College: The Undergraduate Experience in America, New York (1987). Derived data from the WebCASPAR database located at http://webcaspar.nsf.gov/includes/checkJavascriptAbility2.jsp;jsessionid=FFA3F2F865566B6ABFF18381819488C9?submitted=1

"Howard University is the Top Feeder Institution for Black Doctoral Recipients in the sciences and engineering." Journal of Blacks in Higher Education Weekly Bulletin. April 7, 2011.

National Science Foundation, Division of Science Resources Statis- tics. (2010) Science and Engineering Degrees, by Race/Ethnicity of Recipients: 1997–

2006. Detailed Statistical Tables NSF 10-300. Arlington, VA. Available at http://www.nsf.gov/statistics/nsf10300/.

National Science Foundation, National Center for Science and Engineering Statistics. (2011) Women, minorities, and persons with disabilities in science and engineering: 2011. Available at http://www. nsf.gov/statistics/wmpd/pdf/nsf11309.pdf.

National Research Council (1999) Transforming Undergraduate Education in science, mathematics, engineering, and technology. Washington, DC: National Academy Press.

LOUISIANA STATE UNIVERSITY

Su-Seng Pang, Ph.D., Zakiya S. Wilson-Kennedy, Ph.D., Gretchen Burton, Melissa Crawford, Tyrslai M. Williams, Ph.D., and Isiah M. Warner, Ph.D.

Louisiana State University and Agricultural & Mechanical College had its origin in land grants made by the U.S. government in 1806, 1811, and 1827. In 1853, the Louisiana General Assembly established the Seminary of Learning of the State of Louisiana near Pineville, LA. The institution opened in 1860, with Col. William Tecumseh Sherman as superintendent. In 1870, the name of the institution was changed to Louisiana State University. Louisiana State Agricultural & Mechanical College was established by an act of the legislature, approved April 7, 1874, and opened in New Orleans where it remained until it merged with LSU in 1877. The year 1908 marked the formation of the Colleges of Agriculture, arts and sciences, engineering, and education. Dedication of the present campus took place on April 30, 1926. After years of enrollment fluctuation, student numbers began a steady increase, new programs were added, curricula and faculty expanded, and a true state university emerged. LSU has been designated as a land grant, sea grant, and space grant institution. LSU currently includes eleven colleges and six schools, in addition to specialized centers, divisions, institutes, and offices. The University brings in more than $150 million annually in external grants and contracts. LSU's enrollment is currently greater than 30,000 students, including more than 1,600 international students and approximately 5,600 graduate students.

The current institutional commitment to supporting underrepresented minority students in science, technology, engineering, and mathematics at LSU is broad. For example, LSU has emerged as a national model for excellence in awarding Ph.D.s to African Americans in chemistry and engineering. In particular, the Department of chemistry produces more African-American Ph.D.s than any single institution in the Nation. For example, almost nine% of the national production of African-American doctorates in chemistry over the last ten years have graduated from LSU. That's one out of every eleven, which is a remarkable achievement for a single institution.

In addition, sixteen domestic African-American Ph.D. students are currently enrolled in the LSU chemistry Department Graduate Program, and fourteen African-American Ph.D.students graduated from the LSU chemistry Department in the past five years. Professor Isiah M. Warner has been identified as the catalyst for this achievement. Indeed, a unified plan is in place at LSU, including additional prior and planned achievements in the training of minority students, and vigorous recruiting and mentoring efforts are ongoing in all STEM areas.

LSU has a major commitment to increasing campus diversity and improving the success rate of underrepresented segments of the Louisiana population.

Two offices at LSU that relate to issues of campus diversity are the Office of Diversity and the Office of Strategic Initiatives (OSI). OSI is led by Co-PIs Isiah M. Warner, Ph.D., as vice-cpresident and Guoqiang Li, Ph.D., as associate vice-president. Other instrumental OSI leadership team members are Su-Seng Pang, Ph.D., former OSI associate vice president; Zakiya S. Wilson-Kennedy, Ph.D., Former OSI executive assistant and STEM director; Gretchen Schneider, former coordinator; Tyrslai Williams, Ph.D., OSI assistant director; and Melissa Crawford, PI and LS_LAMP manager. (http://osi.lsu.edu).

The Gordon A. Cain Center (http://cain.lsu.edu/) for STEM Literacy provides a third source that reaches out to complement in the area of statewide K-18 education. Among the major roles of all three offices are to aid all students, particularly minority students in STEM fields, to promote shortened periods of time for receiving the B.S. degrees, improved retention rates, recruitment of more statewide high school minority students into STEM areas, and an overall increased minority student pool. In addition, the Cain Center promotes undergraduate educational research in STEM, and provides opportunities for research collaboration and outreach.

Ongoing educational projects associated with OSI and the Cain Center support more than 300 undergraduate and graduate students in STEM disciplines, including many underrepresented students at LSU and numerous high school teachers/students as well as various enhancement activities.

Overall Goals and Objectives

Increase the Number of and Quality of STEM B.S. degrees

The Louis Stokes Louisiana Alliance for Minority Participation Program at Louisiana State University is aimed at substantially increasing the number and quality of minority students enrolled in and completing baccalaureate degrees in STEM and subsequently going on to pursue graduate studies in STEM disciplines. According to the recent External Review, "LSU has been a huge success story for LSU LS-LAMP. Minority STEM bachelor's degrees have grown from forty in the baseline year to 143 in the recent years, a 258% increase."

Increase proportionately the number of LS-LAMP Alumni in STEM graduate Programs

LSU has also emerged as a leader in the matriculation of minority STEM graduates to graduate school. With collaborative efforts with the Office of Diversity, Office of Strategic Initiatives (OSI), and the Gordon A. Cain Center, the LSU LS-LAMP program has put in place the structures necessary to facilitate minority STEM baccalaureate matriculation to graduate school.

Mentoring Activities

LSU mentoring activities can be demonstrated through two types of programs. The first is through the LSU LS-LAMP project, and the second is through all LSU OSI education/research projects. For each activity, the following will be provided: state of activity, goals and objectives, comprehensive implementation strategies with explicit reference to the strands of the Ten-Strand Systemic Mentoring Models, and outcomes.

Mentoring Activities Through LSU LAMP Project

LSU has been a key partner of the LS-LAMP sponsored by the National Science Foundation since 1995. LS-LAMP is a comprehensive statewide program aimed at substantially increasing the number and quality of minority students earning B.S. degrees in STEM disciplines at Louisiana institutions. The LS-LAMP project is based at Southern University, Baton Rouge and involves 12 institutions of higher learning in Louisiana, including LSU. In efforts of achieving the overall goals and objectives, the LSU LS-LAMP program provides activities that follow the Ten-Strand Systemic Mentoring Model developed by the Timbuktu Academy at Southern University and A&M College. The LSU LS-LAMP program provides financial support, communication skill enhancement and computer technology workshops, scientific advisement and research activities, tutoring opportunities, and professional development.

Financial Support

LSU LS-LAMP Undergraduate Scholars are supported during the academic year with various stipends (in average about $1,500 per student) per semester to participate in LS-LAMP activities, including research training. Through LS-LAMP, LSU is also a recipient of six "NSF Louis Stokes Alliance for Minority Participation -- Bridge to the Doctorate Program" (NSF/LS-AMP/BD). Each BD awards 12, two-year Fellowships ($32,000/yr plus tuition and out of state fees) to minority students entering Ph.D. programs in STEM disciplines, who have received their B.S. degrees from LS-AMP institutions.

Communication Skill Enhancement

In collaboration with LSU's Communication across the Curriculum Program, LSU LS-LAMP students have access to various workshops that were aimed at developing the mastery of the English language. CxC is focused on enhancing learning experiences for students and improving their written, spoken, visual presentation, and technological communication skills within the disciplines. The Communication across the Curriculum Program offers communication studios equipped with state-of-the-art technology and highly-skilled communication advisors that support students working on communication-based projects. Each studio provides a host of basic services, including assistance with writing, speaking, visual, and technological communication skills, assignment review and feedback consultations for communication-related projects and video recording of student presentation practice sessions, final presentations, and critiques. As a result, LSU LS-LAMP students have the resources to become skilled leaders and experts in communication.

Comprehensive, Scientific Advisement and Research Activities

LSU LS-LAMP Scholars are provided with ample opportunities that expose them to professional practices and standards. Activities that promote immersion into a professional culture include undergraduate research experience, conference attendance, scientific seminars, reading technical journals and collaboration with others.

Tutoring

The NSF/I3 project, "Integration of Education and Mentoring Programs at Louisiana State University" was an institutional effort designed to integrate a large number of on-going programs at LSU, especially those led by the newly established LSU Office of Strategic Initiatives and LSU's Gordon A. Cain Center for STEM Literacy. The I3 project focused on the following:

1. Consolidation of summer workshops and camps for students, teachers and faculty members;
2. Leadership training in academics through a student-governing organization;
3. High school mathematics tutoring program by college students;
4. Mentoring high school Louisiana science and engineering fair projects by college students; and
5. Integration of research into education in materials engineering and science.

While the I3 project ended in 2014, it was highly effective in integrating numerous education/research projects on the LSU campus, including LSU LS-LAMP, for various activities. In collaboration with the LSU I3 project, select LS-LAMP students assisted with mathematics and science tutoring at East Iberville High School ALEKS Pilot Project; iHope Baton Rouge Desire Street Academy Think Tank Program; Kenilworth Science and Technology Charter School ALEKS Project; Saint Francis Xavier Catholic School Big Buddy Program; and the 100 Black Men ACT Prep Program.

In addition to community outreach tutoring, LS-LAMP students can receive academic tutoring through LS-LAMP sponsored Study Nights and the LSU Center for Academic Success. At the LSU LS-LAMP sponsored Study Nights, tutors are available for

LS-LAMP students in subjects requested by LS-LAMP students. This activity encourages the use of tutors to coach academic excellence and promote peer group learning. The LSU Center for Academic Success provides content-specific assistance with on-campus tutorial centers, online tutoring, and by providing a private tutor for hire list. These resources help students master course content and develop study strategies for specific courses.

Generic Research Activities and Specific Research Projects

Each LS-LAMP Scholar in encouraged to work on a research project under the guidance of an LSU faculty member. By participating in undergraduate research, scholars develop a one-on-one mentoring relationship with faculty members and acquire hands-on experience and general scientific skills that will be valuable for graduate study in the sciences or engineering. Additionally, scholars are encouraged to apply for and participate in summer research experience programs.

Development of a Professional Culture

LS-LAMP Scholars are encouraged to attend national or regional scientific meetings or conferences. LSU has an on-going LSU Summer Undergraduate Research Forum (SURF) in the-Summer and the Excite, Explore, Experiment Undergraduate Research Symposium in the Fall, which invite participation from all LSU Undergraduate Research Scholars. The LS-LAMP Students have the opportunity to present research their research projects and interact with other undergraduate students and Faculty.

In collaboration with LSU IMSD Program, LS-LAMP scholars are encouraged to participate in a research ethics seminar once a semester and attend Scientific Seminars. Ethics training workshops create a foundation to promote Responsible Conduct of

Research. It requires students to think critically about what it means to be an ethical researcher. Below are specific seminars that LS-LAMP scholars attended.

Development of Computer and Technology Skills

The LSU Student Technical, Application and Resource Training Program provided an opportunity for all LSU students to learn and enhance their computer skills to improve their in-class performance, in their jobs, and in their future careers free of charge. The LSU START Program had more than 50 individualized modules from PowerPoint to Advance Webpage design and computer simulations for research. The START program was a collaborative effort between the LSU Center for Academic Success and the Office of Computing Services. The program is no longer active.

As LSU students, LS-LAMP scholars have free access to lynda.com, one of the premier online resources for learning software, technology, business, and creative skills. This resource has been valuable in helping enhance their computer skills, thereby improving their performance in class and in their future careers.

Monitoring and Academic Advising
Guidance to Graduate School

The LSU LS-LAMP program monitors and evaluates student success throughout the academic year. All participants receive academic, career, and personal advising from the program manager Melissa Crawford. The project manager's role is to assist with the Scholars educational training program, as well as to track their academic progress. Depending on the student's academic and personal needs, the students engages in one-on-one sessions at least twice per semester. During these meetings, the student's academic/personal performance is discussed and individualized assessments are made. Additionally, the individual goals of the students are monitored and adapted as needed.

Mentoring activities through LSU OSI
The Louisiana State University Office of Strategic Initiatives was established in 2001. The vision of OSI is to create, leverage, and centralize most education and mentoring programs at LSU. Its missions are to raise students' academic performances as well as to create and implement programs that enhance the diversity of students. The mentoring strategic initiatives include, but are not limited to:
- Developing new mentoring activities;
- Providing funding for potential LSU students, especially for under-represented minorities and females;
- Coordinating efforts to generate education/training grants to support undergraduate students;

- Establishing a close alliance with other universities;
- Supporting K-12 education, teachers, and students;
- Increasing the number of external awards for students; and
- Increasing the number of students (particularly underrepresented) pursuing doctoral degrees.

Over the past eleven years, OSI has exceeded its initial expectations. The LSU/OSI is an innovative endeavor designed to bring in and leverage a large number of student-oriented projects at LSU. Under current leadership, more than forty education/mentoring/research grants have been obtained by OSI since 2001. These grants have generated more than $40 million for students, with more than half of this money involved in on-going projects. Currently, these projects are supporting more than 100 Ph.D. students and 600 undergraduate students (with approximately 51% under-represented minorities and 55% females) as well as hundreds of high school students and teachers.

Mentoring Activities

Summer Bridge Program for Entering STEM Freshmen

OSI facilitated an eight-week Summer Bridge Program from 2006-2012. Each summer, 25-35 newly accepted participants (primarily freshmen) were support by OSI to engage in the bridge program. Students enrolled in up to six hours of courses. The primary purpose of the Summer Bridge Program is to build a community between incoming students and to prepare each one for research and leadership roles at LSU. Participants gain tools needed for success in college. The program also serves as an intensive orientation to LSU and the demands of college coursework, and the expectations of OSI Mentoring Programs are clearly defined. Through their coursework, activities and social programs, the students model an ideal community in terms of friendship, responsibility, diversity, celebration, collaboration, and caring.

Moreover, the participants develop a strong interdependent support network that will reinforce their learning outside the classroom and positively impact their development academically, socially and professionally as undergraduates at LSU and beyond. The OSI Summer Bridge participants, mentors, staff, and parents celebrate at the end of the summer with a reception. The students create and give group presentations about their experiences at Summer Bridge to parents and the LSU administration.

Individual Academic/Research Mentors

In the past, faculty mentors were assigned to the students upon acceptance into the program. Students could elect to either secure research with their assigned mentor, who would serve as both a faculty and research mentor, or secure research independently. To support the goal of developing autonomous scholars, current practice has been to provide the students with the necessary resources for developing effective faculty-student relationships and to encourage them to secure research mentors based on their individual research interests. The program managers provide guidance to the students throughout this process. The faculty mentors attend a training session sponsored by OSI, and each mentor agrees to write his or her student a letter of introduction, and to meet with the student several times per year. The faculty mentors also give research presentations during Summer Bridge as well as during the academic year and attend several program social events and dinners. Additionally, a faculty liaison is identified in each department who will pair the students with mentors, as well as act as a general advocate for OSI Programs in the department.

OSI Summer Research Experience for Undergraduates for Rising Sophomore Students

Undergraduate research has been shown to be strongly correlated with enhancement of the undergraduate education experience, particularly reduced attrition rates and increased rates of graduate education for underrepresented students. OSI has embraced this finding, as all participants are engaged in undergraduate research as early as possible. Furthermore, undergraduate research has been shown to be associated with the attainment of research skills, increased persistence to the undergraduate degree, and influencing the selection of a STEM career. The OSI Summer REU program is developed primarily for rising sophomores. This group of students is targeted because most national REU programs generally recruit junior or senior students. Each year, twenty students are selected. We select students based on the composition of the incoming class of the prior year. The purpose of the OSI Summer REU program is to have students enhance their research skills through their summer experience. The OSI Summer REU program is viewed as more intensive research and is a great foundation for the student's future graduate school research. Additionally, the participants' research experiences enhance their opportunities for graduate school selection.

The primary activity is for students to gain knowledge and develop proper procedures for conducting research. Students are expected to perform research full-time for no less than forty hours per week, for a total of 320 hours within the eight-week session. In addition to individual research, students are required to attend two workshops. The first workshop, "How to Construct a Research Poster," provides detailed instructions for creating research posters and highlights general presentation tips. The second workshop, "Giving Dynamic Poster Presentations," gives detailed information about presenting posters, dressing professionally, and networking. All participants are asked to practice explaining their research in a concise manner. All students are required to present their summer research at the LSU Summer Undergraduate Research Forum at the end of the summer. In an effort to encourage peer mentoring between the REU participants and the OSI Summer Bridge participants, the REU students are required to serve as panel members where they discuss college expectations. Topics include learning strategies, securing undergraduate research, safety, college life, community service, student involvement, and OSI program expectations. Students found the panel to be very beneficial. The OSI REU program grant concluded in 2014.

Newly-Developed Mentoring Courses

OSI developed a series of four university-approved courses focusing on mentoring, education, and research for OSI program students:

- OSI-UC0050 Introduction to Mentoring, Education, and Research (2) F—This course is the first in a series of four designed to increase OSI students' college success and train them as mentors and researchers. The students obtain new learning strategies, explore learning styles, and learn basic research skills. They are mentored by upper-level students and attend research presentations by other students involved in undergraduate research.
- OSI-UC0060 Pursuing Mentoring, Education, and Research (2) S—The second course in the series continues the mentoring, learning strategies, and research exposure from the first course. Students continue to implement the college

success tools gained in UC0050 and gain skills needed to obtain research. Students also assess various applications of terminal degrees in their chosen discipline, develop writing skills necessary for REU application, and engage in peer mentoring.

- OSI-UC0070 Success in Mentoring, Education, and Research (2) F—Students mentor new undergraduates. The course provides support for any problems that they encounter, as well as reinforces what students have learned about research etiquette and ethics. Students gain skills needed for graduate school marketability and preparation, which consists of an extensive GRE preparation workshop. They also continue with community involvement and peer mentoring engagement.
- OSI-UC0080 Advancing in Mentoring, Education, and Research (1) F, S—In the final course, students take on leadership roles as mentors and researchers. In Individual Development Plan (IDP) selections, students at this stage are guided toward larger projects oriented toward research, graduate school preparation/admissions, and career planning.

These four OSI courses reinforce concepts learned in Summer Bridge, provide a setting for peer mentoring relationships, and involve a variety of workshops and guest speakers. The courses provide multiple opportunities for individualization, allowing students to concentrate on improving weaknesses, developing strengths, or exploring new areas of engagement with the guidance of their mentors. All students are matched with peer mentors. The pairs and groups meet during the course to discuss academic, research, and career issues, and are encouraged to communicate outside the course to further develop the relationship. This communication occurs at least two times per semester outside the course.

One core assignment common to all of the courses is the Individual Development Plan, through which students choose assignments relevant to their particular semester goals. A first-year student might choose to complete detailed examinations of all of their tests in one course, to evaluate their time management, to interview a graduate student or faculty member in their field, or to conduct a literature search for their research project. A more advanced student might choose to present a poster at a conference, prepare for the GRE through the Office of Strategic Initiatives GRE Preparation Workshop, to write a scientific article for publication in a journal, or to prepare an application for a national scholarship or fellowship. This process assists them in writing more effective IDP proposals and completes the metacognitive cycle of planning, monitoring, and evaluation. As a whole, the IDP allows students to participate in individualized personal and professional development with some supervision and guidance, modeling an effective system for setting and reaching academic and career goals. The UC Courses have not been offered since 2014, upon the conclusion of two OSI programs.

Individual Mentoring and Counseling

OSI program students are required to meet with OSI staff each semester (minimum of two times per semester for students in good standing). Students on program academic warning or probation are required to meet a minimum of four times per semester. During mentoring meetings, the scholar's academic progress is discussed and students are advised accordingly. Some students require counseling sessions and will meet with the program counselor. When appropriate, students are referred to other resources on campus, including Career Services, the Honors College, the Center for Academic Success, the Writing Center, various on-campus tutorial centers, the Student Health Center, the Center for Freshman Year, and the advising services available through their major colleges. In some instances, the students may also be advised to meet with their professor. Any scholar who receives less than a C on any graded test or paper must seek formal tutoring and verification sheets must be turned in weekly. The program staff monitors the scholar's progress by verifying the completion of the tutoring requirement via mentoring meetings and email correspondence. Students are introduced to learning and study strategies regarding topics such as metacognition, time management, stress, test anxiety, and discipline-specific learning strategies by Saundra Y. McGuire, Ph.D., assistant vice chancellor for learning, teaching, and retention. McGuire is a collaborator on several OSI Mentoring projects, who has published articles and book chapters that help faculty teach in ways that actively engage students in the learning process. The program managers provide guidance to the students throughout this process.

Results of Mentoring

    OSI has supported almost nearly 75% of all underrepresented minority STEM Ph.D. recipients at LSU since 2005. Sixty of LSU minority graduate students have received full fellowships ($32,000 per year for two years plus tuition, out-of-state exemption, special mentoring, etc.), while others have received supplemental fellowships, travel, and other mentoring support. A list of the forty-seven minority Ph.D. students who have received full fellowships from OSI is provided below. Upon completion of the two-year full fellowship, OSI has successfully assisted each individual in their follow-up support (at least $18,000 per year plus tuition) during the remainder of their Ph.D. studies.

Undergraduate Students

LSU/OSI is able to use its grant awards (see Section II) to support and mentor more than 300 undergraduate students in STEM disciplines each year. Students come from all STEM disciplines, including chemistry, biology, physics, computer sciences, mathematics, and all branches of engineering. The students who have received OSI support are quite diversified, as summarized below:

- More than 60% of the students come from under-represented groups.
- Student academic preparation skills are also varied. For example, while some programs are targeted toward high GPA students, OSI has programs which also target low GPA students (under 3.0, as in the HHMI program) whose high school credentials suggest that they should be better students.
- While many programs are merit based, some are also focused on low-income family students.
- Some programs require students to conduct research while others will provide mentoring and training, and all of them require education community services (i.e., K-12 tutoring and teacher assistance).
- Programs that cover academic year or summer or both.
  To date, the annual minority STEM B.S. degree production at LSU has increased more than three-fold from forty degrees in 1994/95 to ~130 per year in recent years.

Retention to Graduation

There has been a vigorous national debate on methodologies for increasing student persistence in STEM undergraduate curricula. Through its mentoring construct, LSU/OSI has been able to dramatically increase the persistence of undergraduate students in STEM disciplines. Moreover, this office has been able to dramatically reduce the graduation gap between majority and minority students. The retention to graduation of three OSI programs has been presented and is compared to national data provided by the Center for Institutional Data Exchange and Analysis. From this alone, it is clear that OSI is a national innovator and leader in educating the next generation of STEM leaders. Notably, 31 OSI have graduated with Latin honors, achieving and sustaining a grade point average of 3.7 or higher.

National Awards

OSI students have received a variety of university and national honors and awards. These include the following:
- Morris K. Udall Scholarship (2)
- Phi Beta Kappa (4)
- NSF Graduate Research Fellowship (4)
- Barry M. Goldwater Scholarship (3)
- Harry S. Truman Scholarship (1)
- HHMI EXROP Scholar (12)
- HHMI Gilliam Fellowship (1)

Demonstration of Student Success

With the mentoring programs developed by OSI, LSU has become a national leader in receiving education and mentoring funds for support of students. Because of all of the grants that OSI has received, hundreds of college students, as well as numerous high school teachers and students, have been supported each year. Among all of the impacts and achievements of OSI, the most significant one is diversity in academia. To demonstrate this impact and benefit, we highlight achievements on diversity below.

For the OSI/LA-STEM Project:

- This project incorporates aspects of the successful Meyerhoff Scholars Program at the University of Maryland, Baltimore County.
- There are currently seventy-seven participants in the Program. All of them are in STEM disciplines with the intention of entering a Ph.D. program upon receiving their B.S. Degree. Among them, 33 are minority participants (African-American, Hispanic, Native American), and thirty-nine are female participants.
- Through the OSI mentoring program, the average cumulative GPA of OSI/LA-STEM Scholars is 3.5/4.0. Since 2006, twenty-three students have received a B.S. degree which includes eight minority participants and ten female participants. Six scholars graduated with university commendation, and 67percent of the graduates have indicated that they have plans to pursue post baccalaureate degrees.
- OSI/LA-STEM Scholars have completed more than 80 presentations (posters and papers), and five publications. OSI/LA-STEM Scholars have received numerous awards and scholarships including the Barry M. Goldwater Scholarship, Truman Scholarship, American Chemical Society Scholarship, Merck Undergraduate Science Research Award Fellowship, and Morris K. Udall Award. (This project expired in 2013.)

For the OSI/HHMI Project:

- This program has focused on recruiting minority students with lower GPAs who show potential for improvement and graduation from the program.
- Thus far, eighty-one Students have been recruited to OSI/HHMI. Among them, sixty-one are African-American/Hispanic, and forty-three are female.
- Five papers have been presented by OSI/HHMI Scholars and three were published. (This project expires in 2016.)

For the OSI/S-STEM Project:

- NSF/S-STEM project is used to support economically disadvantaged students; many of them are underrepresented minorities.
- There are thirty-two students currently being supported by the OSI/S-STEM program.
- Fifty-seven% of the students are Black/Non-Hispanic and 6% are Hispanic. Furthermore, 66% are female.
- While the minimum GPA for entering freshmen is 3.0 and the minimum GPA for currently enrolled LSU students is 2.5, the average GPA of the S-STEM Scholars is 3.451.
- While not mandatory, many of OSI/S-STEM Scholars have presented their research at the Summer Undergraduate Research Forum and several are working on manuscripts with their research advisors. (The project expired in 2017.)

For the OSI/IMSD Project:

- To date, thirty-five students have participated in the OSI/IMSD Program; 85% of them are minority: African-American (25), Hispanic (1), and female students in all races (29).

- All of the above are in STEM disciplines with the intention of entering a graduate program upon receiving their B.S. Degree.
- The average GPA of OSI/IMSD Scholars is 3.3/4.0, and the average number of years for receiving a B.S. degree is 4.2. It takes more than six years for general LSU students to earn a B.S. degree.
- Fourteen papers have been published by OSI/IMSD Scholars.
- OSI/IMSD Scholars have received many Awards, such as the Goldwater Scholarship, Howard Hughes Medical Institute Gilliam Fellowship for Advanced Study, NIH Post Baccalaureate Fellowships, University Medalists, Chancellor's List, and Dean's List. (The program expires Summer 2019.)

For the OSI/LS-AMP/BD and OSI/AGEP/GAELA Project:
- OSI has recruited more than forty-seven minority students in Ph.D. STEM disciplines (chemistry, biological sciences, engineering, etc.).
- The number of minorities in Ph.D. STEM disciplines at LSU is around seventy. Before the establishment of OSI, LSU had only thirty-five.
- OSI has assisted all BD Fellows in receiving additional support after the end of the initial two-year support. This support is generated by OSI through other Fellowships, TA, RA, etc.
- OSI has facilitated LSU chemistry in maintaining the top in African-American Ph.D. Enrollments and Graduates in the nation (22).

- To the credit of OSI, the number of LSU Minority Ph.D. STEM degrees conferred from 2002-03 through 2010-11 is seventy-three (eight-year period).

Conclusion

LSU/OSI and LSU LS-LAMP have been proven as one of the best mentoring units in higher education based on the following indicators:

- The costs for conducting education programs have been leveraged efficiently and effectively;
- More students have been supported;
- Graduation rates have increased;
- More students have received regional/national awards and recognitions; and
- Student performance has improved.

Achieving all of these for college students has been a challenge in higher education, especially for minority and female students in the STEM disciplines. LSU has created numerous innovative mentoring activities to achieve these impressive results. Before the establishment of OSI, each discipline had developed its own set of mentoring programs, resulting in a rigid disciplinary mindset and interpretation of STEM in a narrow context. Barriers between disciplines had resulted in boundaries between the educational/mentoring projects. Therefore, the OSI was established to break disciplinary barriers and change the traditional way of conducting education and mentoring.

We have also leveraged resources available at LSU and enhanced the synergy and positive "composite action" among the existing projects. Mentoring programs have and continue to:

- nurture students in an interdisciplinary environment so that they become inspirational teachers, exemplary mentors, and effective leaders;
- raise academic standing through outstanding achievements by students and faculty;
- create and implement programs that broaden the participation of more diversified students and faculty; and
- enhance the academic environment to better support students, who subsequently transfer their service to K-12 education.

Students must be able to readily relate to a broad spectrum of individuals: academicians, K-12 teachers and students, industry personnel, and the public in general.

It is anticipated that all OSI program students will exert a positive and ethical influence in the community as model citizens. Through all of its devoted effort, OSI is able to (i) educate and mentor students and the community to have sufficient knowledge of what lies across these boundaries; (ii) innovatively integrate all education and mentoring summer programs for college faculty and students as well as high school teachers and students; (iii) provide a higher level of leadership training for students; (iv) integrate and leverage the STEM research between college and high school students; (v) establish a mechanism for college students to volunteer their efforts in tutoring high school students. More information regarding the transformative programs housed within the OSI can be found in literature. (Crawford 2018; Williams)

References

Crawford, M.B., Wilson-Kennedy Z. S., Thomas, G.A., Gilman, S.D. & Warner, I.M. (2018) "LA-STEM research scholars program: A model for broadening diversity in STEM education." Technology & Innovation, 19(3), 577-592.

LS-LAMP Best Practices in Systemic STEM Mentoring

Williams, T.M., Crawford, M.B., Hooper-Bui, L.M, S., Lavender, H., Watt, S, & Warner, I.M. LSU Office of Strategic Initiatives: A Great Equalizer for Broadening Participation in STEM (Accepted).

BEST PRACTICES IN SYSTEMIC STEM MENTORING AT MCNEESE STATE UNIVERSITY

George Mead, Ph.D., and Darreen Alcock

The McNeese Summer Bridge Program is a summer semester Academic Support Program. Participants earn seven hours of college credit in courses like college algebra, pre-calculus, trigonometry, and freshmen foundations, while becoming acclimated to campus life and university services by living in campus housing. High school graduates who plan to pursue a bachelor's degree in science, technology, engineering, or mathematics at McNeese State University can participate in the summer LS-LAMP program offered to STEM majors through the College of Science. These students must enroll in and pursue a four-year degree at McNeese. The major goal of this program is to increase the number of underrepresented groups of students receiving baccalaureate and graduate degrees in science, technology engineering, and mathematics. The Program encourages African American, Hispanic American Indian, and Pacific Islanders to apply. Students will be selected for the six-week program which includes textbooks, tuition, and fees, housing and summer meal plan. Students who successfully complete this program will receive college credit for the courses offered through this program. These students may also receive a stipend for up to $1,000, based on their performance in the program.

Financial Support

College of Science Summer Bridge Program

Students were selected for the six-week program will receive financial support through tuition, and fees, housing and summer meal plan. Students who successfully complete this program will receive college credit for the courses offered through this program. These students may also receive a stipend up to $1,000, based on their performance in the program. Participants were provided employment opportunities in specialized academic areas in the College of Science Tutoring Center, as Math Lab tutors in the Department of Mathematics College Algebra Math Lab, as computer technicians in the Academic Computing Center, and as peer mentors in the Summer Bridge Program.

Tutoring

LS-LAMP participants were employed as Peer Mentors in the McNeese Summer Bridge Program. LS-LAMP Peer Mentors helped summer Bridge students become acclimated to college life, by living with them the dorm, peer advising, and being peer tutors. LS-LAMP Participants were employed in the College of Science Tutoring Center housed in Kirkman Hall. LS-LAMP students were designated as specialized tutors to help at-risk students achieve academic success. Five scholars and affiliate scholars worked as tutors or peer mentors.

Research Activities

Participants received hands-on undergraduate research experiences in areas of their academic fields. LS-LAMP students were able to participate in the McNeese Faculty Colloquium. LS-LAMP participants were encouraged to become engaged in professional organizations, attend seminars and conferences, and become involved in research. LS-LAMP scholars Devin Norman and Lucretia Edwards presented at conferences during the 2012-2013 academic year with Charles Watson, Ph.D. Fourteen scholars and other affiliates worked on research in various academic areas during the year.

Development of Professional Culture

In the research component of the Summer Bridge Program, Charles Watson, Ph.D., exposed LS-LAMP scholars to ideas of ethics in research, the readings of journals and related papers as well as a discussion on joining professional societies in their current academic area.

Development of Computer and Technological Skills

Scholars are encouraged in their Freshmen Foundations course to surf the web for productive research opportunities. In this course they are required to present projects using word-processing, graphics and spreadsheets. LS-LAMP Scholars are given employment opportunities as computer technicians in the Academic Computing Center. Fourteen scholars and affiliate scholars received computer and technological skills throughout the school year.

Monitoring

LS-LAMP scholars are assigned an academic advisor in their respective discipline. LS-LAMP Peer Mentors helped Summer Bridge students become acclimated to college life, by living with them in the dorm, peer advising, and being peer tutors.

Guidance to Graduate School

LAMP participants were enrolled in the Freshmen Foundations course designed to enhance their skills in the first years of college and beyond. All LS-LAMP scholars successfully completed the course during the Summer Bridge Program.

BEST PRACTICES IN SYSTEMIC STEM MENTORING AT NUNEZ COMMUNITY COLLEGE

Christine Thomas, Gillian McKay, and Stephen Waddell

Nunez Community College is a comprehensive community college offering general education and occupational technologies curricula that blend the humanities, social sciences, and natural sciences and lead to associate degrees, certificates, and workforce development opportunities. Nunez is located just south of New Orleans in Chalmette, Louisiana. Current enrollment of the college is approximately 2,400 students per semester. The student population is currently 67% female and 33% male. The average age of our students falls between 18 and 29 years of age. Nunez serves Orleans, Jefferson, St. Bernard, St. Tammany, and Plaquemines parishes in south Louisiana. Ethnicity and Race breakdown of the college is as follows: 52% Caucasian, 37% African American, 2% Asian, 1% American Indian, and less than 1% Native Hawaiian or Pacific Islander, two or more races, or un-known race.

Nunez is separated into three major departments within the college. Business and technology holds 24% of our students, Health and Natural sciences holds 21% of our students, and Arts and Humanities holds 19% of our students. The remaining 38% of our students includes high school dual enrollment students and those not currently seeking a degree from the college. In the spring of 2011, for which we have the most updated data, we had a total of 267 students in LS-LAMP majors. At Nunez, this is LA Transfer Associate of science in biology or chemistry, computer science, or process technology (pre-engineering). Of those 267,111 were minorities.

Overall Goals and Objectives

The overall goal of the Nunez Community College LS-LAMP program is to increase the number of students transferring to a four year institution. As the only community college included in the LS-LAMP program in the State of Louisiana, we are chal-lenged everyday to see our students move toward continuing their education rather than go directly into the workforce. The need for our students to work is very high as they come into our institution with families to support and other debts from life. The draw to receive a paycheck, though it may be smaller because of an associate degree, is still more promising to the majority of our students than it is to put off a paycheck in pursuit of an advanced degree and greater reward at the end. Nunez is proud to report that we had sixteen students transfer for the 2010-2011 academic school year, when we only reported five the previous academic year. We believe this increase is because of Nunez's efforts with the Ten-Strand Systemic Mentoring Model. Our efforts are defined below.

Financial Support

Nunez Community College provides support to minority students in the form of scholarships. The student must be completing full-time course work in one of the disciplines mentioned previously, and must maintain a 3.0 or higher GPA. These scholarships are offered in conjunction with other Financial Aid offered by the college, specifically Title IV funds, PELL grants, Federal loans, and TOPS. The goal of this activity is to allow a student to complete coursework and to create a feeling of financial stability great enough for them to maintain a full-time course load. With the barriers discussed above, it can be difficult to maintain a full-time schedule and a family without working full time, as well. We feel these scholarships assist in that endeavor.

In order to promote the availability of the scholarships, the Nunez LS-LAMP staff hosts orientation sessions (two in the fall and one in the spring) to introduce LS-LAMP to those students that may qualify. All students who are minorities and are enrolled in the disciplines discussed receive an invitation to attend the orientation. A brief presentation is given to the students about the scholarship itself, as well as activities and services available to them as LS-LAMP scholars. Each student also receives a certificate of recognition to show their participation in the program.

These activities have greatly increased inquiries into the program, and we have received a number of requests for scholarships than we had previously received prior to implementing the orientation sessions. For the 2011-2012 academic year, we had 10 students receive scholarships through LS-LAMP. In previous years, we usually had no more than five students receiving the scholarship. Promotion of the program has given Nunez the opportunity to assist more students with both their current endeavors, as well as their ability to transfer with less debt.

Communication Skill Enhancement

Besides required general English and Speech courses for every major on campus, Nunez offers several opportunities for the students to become more confident in communication. Each student who receives a scholarship through LS-LAMP must first present an essay to the LS-LAMP Coordinators discussing their goals, why they chose the major that they chose, and their intentions for continuing their education beyond Nunez. All essays are expected to use proper grammar, sentence and paragraph structure, spelling, and punctuation. Also, several lectures on various topics are given throughout the academic year.

Nunez has a monthly history lecture series that covers various historical topics dealing with New Orleans and Louisiana. We also have begun a series of lectures in Multiculturalism. We have had guest appearances from a Mardi Gras Indian Tribe and a discussion of the importance of the African American community in the development of popular music in the United States. All students are welcome at these lectures.

Students are given the opportunity to speak publicly outside of the classroom with our Free Speech Alley program. This program is held once a semester and gives the students the opportunity to voice their opinions on local, statewide, and national current events. Any student may speak and must be prepared to answer any question or rebuttal from the audience of their peers. Though a more casual atmosphere, this activity gives the student an opportunity to practice speaking publicly when they may not normally have the opportunity to do so.

Finally, all students who are LS-LAMP Level One scholars (students who receive financial assistance through LS-LAMP) are required to submit work samples at the end of each semester. They are required to submit a clean copy of one paper and/or project from each of their credit classes. The requirement to submit at the end of the semester allows for the student to submit their best work. In this capacity, they are working to create meaningful portfolios of their work to be utilized as they see fit after they leave the college. For all writing samples submitted, they must follow all grammar, sentence and paragraph structure, spelling, and punctuation guidelines of the English language. They also must follow citation guidelines as laid about by their instructors. Most instructors follow MLA guidelines.

Comprehensive, Scientific Advising

All students upon admittance to the college are assigned an advisor within their department. Also, all advisors are instructed to follow strict procedures to insure students are moving through the curriculum as effectively as possible. Students meet with an advisor during designated advising periods throughout the year. A graduation checklist is completed on each student and is updated at the end of each semester once grades are issued. This enables the advisor to enroll students in the next level of courses. Through this process, we have gained a greater number of students completing credentials as the advisor is aware of when a student is meeting a milestone within their degree.

Tutoring

All LS-LAMP Level One scholars at Nunez are required to serve as a tutor or mentor to their peers. They are required to complete five hours a month for all full months within the semester. The tutoring can be formal or informal, as long as it is documented. The LS-LAMP staff also makes the faculty aware that these students are available as necessary. We find that this helps our students become more visible on campus and it leads to other leadership and service roles within the college community. It also helps other students not only within their classes but they become more aware of the LS-LAMP program and the visibility for the program is increased.

All LS-LAMP Level One scholars also sign contracts when they first meet with a LS-LAMP Coordinator that they themselves will seek out tutoring in specific disciplines when needed. Currently, we have full time Learning Specialists on campus for mathematics and English.

For other disciplines, it is recommended to the students to seek out additional help from faculty or to become a part of a study group for peer learning opportunities. The LS-LAMP Coordinators assist students with locating a tutor if the faculty member cannot assist the student in that capacity. We find that making ourselves available as Coordinators to the students and assisting the students in finding tutoring/peer learning opportunities garners more confidence in the student to seek out those opportunities on their own. They utilize more services on campus and become more productive students as a whole.

Generic Research Activities

As previously discussed, all LS-LAMP Level One students are required to submit work samples at the end of each semester. If a class requires a research project, we request of the students that the work for that project be submitted as their work sample. As LS-LAMP coordinators, we encourage the use of effective research practices to complete this work. Students are encouraged to attend research presentations as often as they are available. The LS-LAMP coordinators have provided assistance to attend two recent opportunities for this. The first was in the fall of 2011 at Louisiana State University. One student attended the LSU Research Symposium as a guest. He was able to attend poster presentations as well as oral presentations to gain experience in the presentation side of research.

The University of New Orleans and their LS-LAMP department hosted an informational session for Nunez students who were interested in transferring. Ashok Puri, Ph.D., LS-LAMP coordinator for UNO, gathered several students currently at UNO who had begun their education at a community college. He also asked those students to discuss their experience with research. The students were able to hear positive experiences about research which was also very encouraging to our students. Two of the students who attended the presentation are already in the process of transferring to UNO.

Specific Research Project Execution

Nunez LS-LAMP scholars have been involved in two separate research activities that have given them specific research experience. Two of our LS-LAMP Level One Scholars participated in the Summer Research Internship at the University of New Orleans in 2011. Both received hands-on research experience in a setting outside of their comfort zone of Nunez Community College. Both served under the guidance of a professor as part of a research team and received valuable experience in research. The project topics were Thermo-electric Properties of Nanostructred BI 2-x TE 3+x and Evidence for Non-Conventional Intramolecular Hydrogen Bonds in the Molecular Structure of B-Thymine.

With the experience they received, as well as the financial support, they both were able to transfer successfully to a four-year institution within their discipline. During the 2011-2012 academic year, the Nunez Community College environmental science courses partnered with the Tulane School of Public Health to complete testing on waste water at several local water treatment facilities along the Mississippi River.

The goal of the project is to ultimately be able to reroute waste water into the wetlands in order to rebuild them. Two of our LS-LAMP Level One students were enrolled in these courses and were able to participate. This also gives direct research experience while also giving our students opportunities to address local environmental needs.

Development of a Professional Culture

As previously stated, students are encouraged to attend research presentations as much as possible to gain experience with how students should conduct themselves within a research setting. Nunez also holds workshops on campus that encourage a professional culture. Previous topics have included time management, financial health, successful social media practices, and classroom etiquette. All students on campus whether they are a participant of the LS-LAMP program or not are invited to attend. Also, all LS-LAMP Level One scholars are required to submit a resume to be kept in their file. This gives the student an understanding of why they are attending school in the first place, which is to become a professional, productive member of society.

Development of Computer and Technological Skills

All students are required to complete a survey course in computer skills. The course teaches proper use of word processing, the Internet and web browsing, e-mail usage, and other computer operations necessary for successful entry into this technological world. In other courses submitted work that is greater than a homework assignment or quiz is required to be typed. Usage of online scholarly databases is encouraged for research and other projects. These databases are available at every computer on campus and every registered student has access to them at an off campus site with proper login information. This has resulted in a culture on campus that is technology centered to best prepare our students for today's workforce.

Monitoring

Monitoring is completed on every LS-LAMP scholar throughout the semester. If midterm grades are below expectations, they are discussed with the student to determine the best course of action. They are made aware several times throughout the semester that if grades fall below the required GPA that their scholarship will be in jeopardy. Also, at the beginning of the semester all class schedules are discussed to insure that all students are going to be successful. If one of the Coordinators feels that a student is enrolled in classes they may not be successful with, a meeting is held with the student to discuss it.

The ultimate goal is to keep the student on track to graduate in a timely fashion. Folders are also kept on each student. The folders include class schedules, portfolio and work samples, a resume, and other pertinent documents to the LS-LAMP program. The folders are very helpful in monitoring the student's progress. The coordinators can look at work completed to insure students grasp the concepts learned within their courses. If work turned in is not deemed to be the student's best work, they will be asked to sit for a meeting to discuss how the work can be improved in the following semester. This also serves as a good opportunity to discuss with the student what level of work will be expected at the next level of their education.

Guidance to Graduate School

Though we are a two year institution, Nunez highly encourages our LS-LAMP participants whether receiving scholarships or not to transfer to four-year institutions and eventually on to graduate school. In the past, we have found that barriers to transfer from Nunez mainly come from a fear of being on an unfamiliar campus. Nunez, as well as other two-year institutions, can become very comfortable to an individual, and they often do not have the courage to continue their education in another place. The LS-LAMP coordinators determined that an effective way to break this fear would be to take the students to these campuses. We provide transportation to no less than five different campuses during the academic year. The visits can be general campus tours, meeting one-on-one with faculty within the STEM departments, and meeting other students who are just like them. Being on the campus with others they are familiar with has been beneficial.

Also, learning about the wide range of opportunities for transfer students has been very encouraging for those that may not have taken the time to research them on their own. As previously discussed, we greatly increased our numbers of students transferring, and we believe these campus visits have directly contributed to that. Once the student has decided to transfer, the LS-LAMP coordinators assist the students with guidance in completing applications and other documents required by the four year institution. Students can meet with either coordinator one on one to assist in completion of the application and also to have the Coordinator proofread and make suggestions on essays and questions answered. The students can also receive reimbursement for application fees once proof is shown that an application has been submitted. We find this has also assisted in increasing our numbers of students transferring.

Conclusion

Nunez Community College students have benefitted greatly from the LS-LAMP scholarship program. The numerous opportunities that have been discussed have greatly increased awareness of what is available to our students after completion of a two-year degree. We have more students interacting within the LS-LAMP program, and those that have received scholarships are proud to discuss their involvement with the program. Without this program, many students would not have transferred due to financial instability, fear, and lack of encouragement. LS-LAMP has given many of our students confidence that they can be successful and productive members of society no matter where they came from. Nunez looks forward to many more students accomplishing these goals through this program.

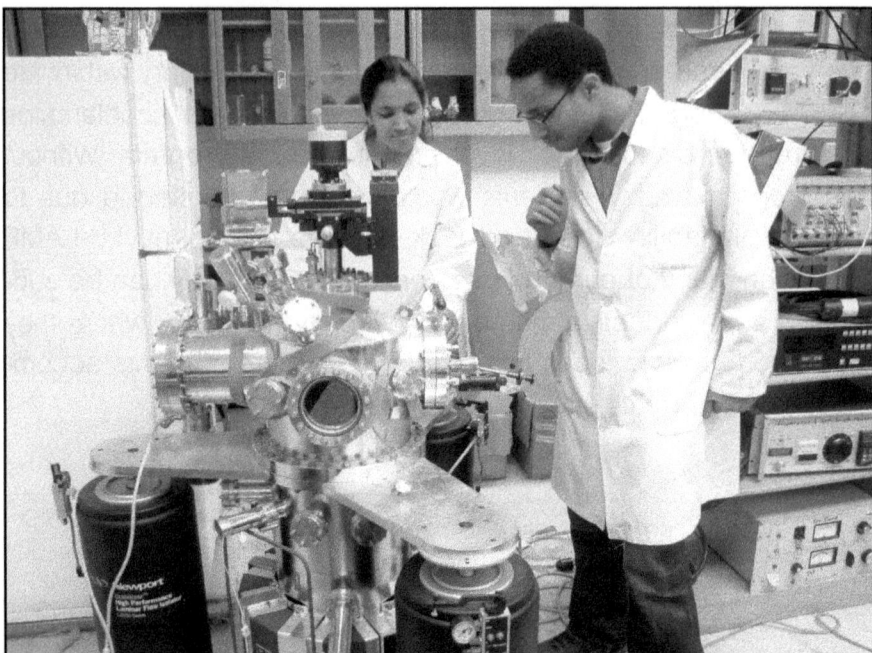

BEST PRACTICES IN SYSTEMIC STEM MENTORING AT SOUTHERN UNIVERSITY AND A&M COLLEGE

Ella Kelley, Ph.D, Lashounda Franklin, Eleanor Collins, and Diola Bagayoko, Ph.D

Southern University and Agricultural and Mechanical College in Baton Rouge (SUBR), Louisiana, is the lead institution for the Louisiana Senior Alliance. The Statewide Program Office is housed at SUBR, in the Department of Mathematics and Physics. Diola Bagayoko, Ph.D., LS-LAMP principal investigator and projector director, serves as campus coordinator. The Ella L. Kelley, Ph.D., serves as LS-LAMP co-principal investigator and campus coordinator. Lashounda Franklin serves as the LS-LAMP senior research associate.

Through the synergistic efforts of the Timbuktu Academy and LS-LAMP at SUBR, students have been immersed in the US Presidential Award-winning 10-Strand Systemic Mentoring Model. The Timbuktu Academy (http://www.phys.subr.edu/timbuktu.htm) is a national model program for the systemic mentoring of undergraduate students, including research participation, and for pre-college outreach and enrichment. SUBR has ten science, technology, engineering, and mathematics (STEM) departments. Since 1997, SUBR has funded the quarter-time release for a departmental mentoring coordinator (DMC) in each of these ten units. In what follows, we present a brief history of Southern University and A&M College along with its mission. We then give quantitative results of our successful implementation of the systemic mentoring model on SUBR's campus and beyond.

Brief History of SUBR

SUBR is one (1) of five (5) campuses within the Southern University System. Established in 1974, the Southern University System is comprised of institutions under the supervision and management of the Board of Supervisors. Southern University opened its doors in 1880, in New Orleans, Louisiana, with 12 students, five (5) faculty members, and a total budget of $10,000. In 1914, it moved to its current location on the banks of the Mississippi River, in Baton Rouge, Louisiana. As a Land Grant College, the mission of SUBR encompasses quality instruction, research, and service. SUBR presently has seven (7) colleges, including that of Sciences and Engineering (CSE). Programs that are aimed at enhancing the overall learning and growth experiences of students are the D. M. R. Spikes Honors College, the Timbuktu Academy and LS-LAMP (www.subr.edu/lslamp). LS-LAMP is modeled after the Timbuktu Academy and they both recruit STEM majors only. At Southern, we celebrate academic achievements, research, athleticism, diversity, and our solemn history. SUBR prepares its students to be leaders, productive citizens, and competitive, both professionally and socially, for the national and international job markets.

In what follows, we discuss a few quantitative results in terms of degree attainment before discussing the strands of our model, one at a time. We then conclude with a summary of our participants' international research experiences.

LS-LAMP and the Timbuktu Academy at SUBR

Through the collaborative efforts of LS-LAMP and the Timbuktu Academy at SUBR, students have been immersed in the US Presidential Award Winning Ten-Strand Systemic Mentoring Model described elsewhere in this document. The provision of financial assistance, scientific advisement, communication skills enhancement, tutoring activities, and generic scholarly (or research) activities are the first five (5) strands of the model. The last five (5) are the execution of specific scholarly (or research) projects, immersion in a professional culture, technical and technological skills enhancement, monitory (in part with a portfolio), and guidance to graduate school or to the job market. These overlapping and complementary strands serve to ensure the integration of a student academically, socially, and professionally, with the aim of becoming a superior learner and a critical thinker. In so doing, the implementation of this systemic mentoring directly addresses the goals and objectives of LS-LAMP, i.e., to increase the number and quality of underrepresented minorities (URM) earning Bachelor degrees in science, technology, engineering, and mathematics (STEM); to promote the successful graduate enrollment of a large proportion of these alumni; and to offer international research and experiential learning for the scholars and to institutionalize best practices.

Established a few years before LS-LAMP in 1990, the goals and objectives of the Timbuktu Academy for college STEM majors are perfectly aligned with the first two (2) of LS-LAMP as spelled out above. These two (2) are increasing the number and quality of URM's earning Bachelor degrees in STEM and the promotion of graduate school attendance by this alumni. Consequently, from 1995 to present, LS-LAMP and the Timbuktu Academy have synergistically implemented our systemic mentoring model for the benefit of STEM majors at SUBR.

As per the Power Law of Human Performance [1-3] and its extension [4], the Law of Human Performance, we know, as opposed to just believing, that all students can learn and excel in STEM. This same law shows that in the genesis of educational, research, and professional value-added, there are no substitutes for exposure to the appropriate subject and materials, at the appropriate scope and depth, and the deploying of adequate efforts to practice and master their knowledge and skill content –preferably in a supportive, engaging, and challenging environment.

Through LS-LAMP and the Academy, more than three hundred (300) minority undergraduate scholars have earned a Bachelor of Science degree from SUBR. Seventy-eight percent (78%) of ninety-four physics graduates, 70% of fifty-four chemistry graduates, and 31% of eighty engineering graduates have earned STEM graduate degrees or are successfully enrolled in graduate school, with an emphasis on the pursuit of the Ph.D. These graduate degrees are mostly masters of science (MS) degrees and philosophy doctorate in the applicable STEM disciplines or directly related ones even though some have earned jurist doctorates (JD) and medical doctorates (MD). Their competitiveness is borne out by their admission in excellent graduate programs with full financial support. Over a fourteen-year span (1995-2009), 10% of all African Americans who earned the Ph.D. degree in Physics or directly related fields are alumni of SUBR. The same full-time dedication to scholarly pursuit explains the reasons eleven scholars have been student grand marshals of SUBR between 2002 and 2012. We should note that these alumni who attended graduate school obtain substantial graduate fellowships and assistantships based on their academic and research credentials. Our results, particularly the ones for the competitive research training of our scholars, have earned the Academy, LS-LAMP, and their directors two US Presidential Awards for Excellence in Science, Mathematics, and Engineering Mentoring (US-PAESMEM) in 1996 and 2002, the Benjamin Banneker Legacy Award in 2007, and the Lifetime Mentor Award of the American Association from the Advancement of Science in 2010. The above results for undergraduate minority STEM majors are made possible by a host of activities in the strands of our model, as partly elucidated below.

Best Practices In Systemic Mentoring
Illustrative Program Results

In what follows, we provide quantitative results of our successful implementation of the Ten-Strand Systemic Mentoring Model. These results are presented in a context that indicates activities that ensure their attainment. Table 1 gives a concise listing of the numbers of scholars who have participated in the implementation of the various strands of our model, from 2000 to 2012. It is important to mention that the numbers of scholar participants, in the table, are not necessarily for distinct students, as some scholars attend more than one conference and others make more than one presentation in the same year.

For the last twelve years, 603 scholars received financial support from LS-LAMP. The ones from Louisiana, with an American College Test (ACT) score over the State's average, receive free tuition through the State's Taylor (Tuition) Opportunity Program for Students (TOPS). Scholars are encouraged to seek additional financial support, if needed, from the university, their college or department, and other sources. By design, the financial support for most scholars is from diversified sources. The aim is to meet all the financial needs associated with matriculation at SUBR, so as to avoid long hours at odd jobs. In so doing, the full-time occupation of most scholars is studying, research, and limited volunteerism. Consequently, they avail themselves to the proper execution of the remaining nine (9) strands of our systemic mentoring model, beginning with scientific advisement and tutoring.

Table 1. Quantitative List of Scholars who Participated in the Systemic Mentoring Activities, from 2000 to 2012

Systemic Mentoring Activities	Number of Participants
Scholars Who Received Financial Assistance	603
Scholars Who Received Scientific Advisement	1031
Scholar Participants in Peer Tutoring and Volunteerism Efforts	641
Scholar Participants in Communication Skills Enhancement	641
Scholar Participants in Generic (Academic Year) Research	668
Scholar Participants in Summer Research Internships (at 269 distinct sites)	384
Scholar Attendees at 184 Conferences	1503
Scholars' Presentations at Conferences	696
Scholar Attendees of Weekly Seminars	1031
Scholar Participants in Continuing Education for Emerging Computer and Other Technologies	1031
Scholars Engaged in Monitoring	1031
Scholars Engaged in Guidance to Graduate School or the High Technology Job Market	1031

Numbers include those of LS-LAMP and Timbuktu Academy scholars and of affiliate STEM students. Numbers of participants are not necessarily those of distinct students, as some scholars attend more than one conference in the same year. Similarly, some presentations, in the same year, are not necessarily made by distinct scholars.

From 2000 to 2012, faculty and staff members advised 1031 scholars; this number does not necessarily represent that of distinct students. Without proper advisement, our experience shows that some students needlessly fail to graduate in four (4) years. Taking courses out of sequence, enrolling in courses that do not count toward graduation, and taking language classes not in the university required sequence are among the errors made by self-advised students. A component of our advisement consists of ensuring students' understanding of the Law of Human Performance [4] in order not to conclude a lack of adequate intelligence due to difficulties in a course. Said difficulties, more often than not, result from missing background necessary for understanding the material-particularly in STEM disciplines with a rigid or taxonomic, internal structure. A significant number of Level 2 students benefit from this scientific advisement, even though they do not receive direct LS-LAMP financial support.

Once a student is in their proper courses, the task is to ensure superior learning, which is partly enabled by tutoring. While freshmen and sophomores are generally tutees, juniors and seniors often serve as tutors. We make it clear that being a tutee is to ensure superior learning, as opposed to engaging in remedial operations. Time management and study skills enhancement are a part of our extended tutoring efforts. Participation in this tutoring is required for Level 1 scholars, i.e., the ones directly supported with LS-LAMP funds. As per the content of the table above, 641 scholars have been engaged in peer tutoring and volunteerism efforts at the University and in their communities. In particular, our scholars serve as tutors in STEM departments, in the SUBR Athletics Department, in their communities, and for professional organizations. Let us note here that serving as tutors in STEM areas is a way to practice ones' STEM subject for mastering it, as

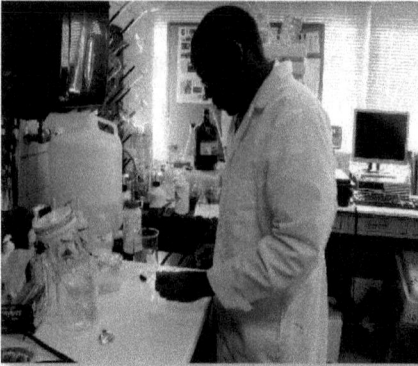

per the Law of Human Performance. The organizations served by these scholar tutors include the Urban and Rural Community Design Research Center, the Boys and Girls Club, Volunteers in Public Schools, the American Red Cross, the Salvation Army, Alpha Phi Alpha Fraternity Inc., Delta Sigma Theta Sorority Inc., the Susan G. Komen Breast Cancer Foundation, Phi Beta Sigma Fraternity Inc., the St. Vincent de Paul Soup Kitchen, Alpha Kappa Alpha Sorority Inc., and Court Appointed Special Advocates (CASA). Our scholars also volunteer as program representatives to recruit qualified and purposeful students into LS-LAMP and the Timbuktu Academy.

We stress to the scholars that there is no substitute for good communication skills (i.e., listening, speaking, reading and writing). We contend that superior communication skills promote superior learning and research, on the one hand, and professional advancement in most careers, on the other hand. From 2000 to 2012, 641 scholars have partaken in our communication skills enhancement. These efforts include weekly seminar sessions devoted to our hand-out on "English Grammar and Usage," and two (2) other hand-outs on "Preparing and Making an Oral or a Poster Presentation," and "Writing a Technical Report, Manuscript, or Thesis." As per the content of Table 1, hundreds of students have attended conferences (to see models of presentations) and hundreds have, themselves, made presentations, as a way of practicing communication skills while disseminating research findings.

A total of 668 scholars have conducted generic research during the academic year. Generic research activities include (1) rigorous literature searches on various subjects and databases, using sophisticated search algorithms and related iterations; (2) current awareness readings, particularly on science and techno- logical developments; (3) discussions of the fine structures of the scientific method; and (4) creative and critical thinking. Several faculty members require their advisees to prepare oral presenta- tions or to write technical reports on topics of their choice. As a way of cultivating communication skills germane to success in research. These skills are brought to bear during students' sum- mer research internships.

From 2000 to 2012, 384 scholars were competitively selected to conduct summer research at laboratories around the country at 269 distinct locations. These summer research sites include the Massachusetts Institute of Technology, the University of North Texas Health Science Center, Cincinnati Children's Hospital, Texas Tech Universi- ty, Kansas State Uni- versity, the Mayo Clinic, the University of Alabama, Meharry Medical School, the National Institute of Standards and Technology, Merck Research Laborato- ries, Noland and

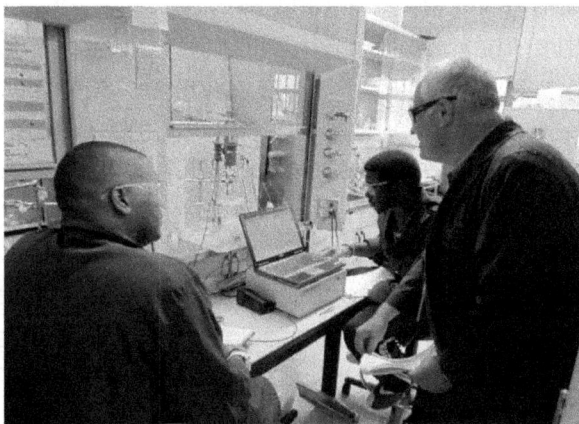

Wang Architectural Center, the University of South Alabama Mitchell Cancer Institute, Iowa State University, Louisiana State University, Morgan State University, Arkansas Center for Space and Planetary Sciences at the University of Arkansas, the University of Chicago, the California Institute of Technology, the University of Kentucky, and Johns Hopkins University, just to name a few. Naturally, our scholars have conducted summer research at several national laboratories including those of NASA and DOE. The most popular federal research sites are Los Alamos, Lawrence Livermore, Brookhaven, and Fermi National Laboratories, and NASA Goddard and Marshall Space Flight Centers. All summer research interns have to make a technical presentation and write and submit a technical report. Needless to say, presentations and reports are critical in a research career. While all our scholars conduct research in the academic year or the summer before graduation, an increasing number of them acquire international research experience, as described in another section farther below.

The immersion in a professional culture has several dimensions. Attending conferences, making technical presentations, and regularly attending seminars are three (3) different aspects of this immersion, in addition to the conduct of research as described above. In what follows, we provide quantitative results and proven best practices for the successful immersion of our scholars in a professional culture.

As a means of effectively enhancing their communication skills, scholars are required to attend and/or present either their summer or academic year research findings at conferences across the nation. Specifically, 1,503 scholars attended 184 conferences around the country, from 2000 to 2012. A total of 696 of these scholars made technical presentations at these conferences. These national conferences include those of the National Society of Black Physicists (NSBP), the Thurgood Marshall College Fund Leadership, and the National Emerging Researchers (ERN). They also attend the Annual Biomedical Research Conference for Minority Students (ABRCMS), and annual conferences of Beta Kappa Chi and the National Institute of Science (BKX/NIS), the Society of Toxicology (SOT), and the American Physical Society (APS).

A total of 1,031 scholars were immersed in a professional culture by attending at least 30 weekly seminars per academic year, which do not include additional meetings with visiting professors and undergraduate and graduate school recruitment sessions. As per the 10-Strand Systemic Mentoring Model, scholars were required to attend weekly seminars. These seminars address (1) GRE preparation, (2) guidance to and funding for graduate school, (3) elements of professional conduct and development, (4) professional information processing (5) ethics in science, (6) special STEM topics from visiting scholars, and (7) opportunities for academic year research or summer research internships.

Specific content of seminar presentations by the campus coordinator include "The Power Law and The Law of Human Performance [4]," "Accuracy, Precision, Completeness, Coherence, and Clarity (APC3) as Basic Characteristics of Critical Thinking and Professional Information Processing," "Thought, Emotion, and Action Management (TEAM)," "Ethics in Science," and "A Problem Solving Paradigm [5]." Other topics were noted in connection with our discussion on communication skills enhancement. Scholars are urged to apply the aforementioned concepts in their academic, professional, and social en-

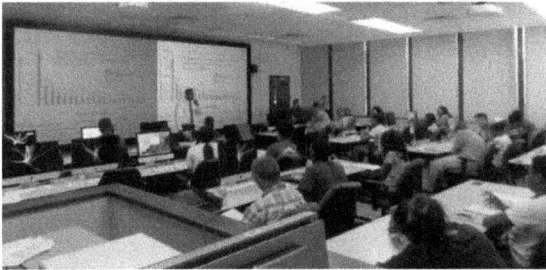

deavors on a regular basis. As per the Law of Human Performance, it is only through regular practice that these concepts will be internalized to induce good habits.

The continued **scientific and technological development** strongly indicate that life-long learning is a necessity in this 21st Century. The emergence of the internet is only a few decades in the past. Cloud, analytics, mobility, social and security (CAMSS) are presently unavoidable components of best practices in most competitive industries. That was not the case a few decades ago. The deoxyribonucleic acid (DNA) editing power of Clustered Regularly Interspaced Short Palindromic Repeats (CRISPR) portent momentous development in biological and medical spheres in the next few decades. These three (3) illustrations indicate the necessity for a scholar to continue the acquisition of emerging skills and to develop working knowledge of new technologies pertinent to their field. Fortunately, at their summer research sites, most scholars are exposed to state of the art technologies and practices in their fields.

Our **comprehensive monitoring** of current and former scholars includes the maintenance and updating of a mentoring portfolio for each scholar. This portfolio includes the scholar's program application, letters of recommendation, resume, personal statement, student data form, LS-LAMP Scholars' and Departmental Mentors' Interaction and Verification form, transcript, ACT scores (for incoming freshmen), technical academic and summer research reports, and weekly seminar quizzes. Our scholars are required to submit updated versions of the aforementioned forms each semester. It is important to note that scholars are required to meet with their respective DMC each semester so that they can receive comprehensive, scientific advisement. This **advisement** ensures that the scholar is following their respective undergraduate curriculum by properly sequencing their courses. These sessions are documented on the LS-LAMP Scholars' and Departmental Mentors' Interaction and Verification form. This advisement effortlessly follows the balance sheets for the various degree programs. Specifically, all the courses for the majors and all the other university required courses are listed on these balance sheets, along with applicable electives. These balance sheets are also factored into the Individual Development Plan (IDP) for each student. The portfolio is a pivotal factor in ensuring the comprehensiveness of our exemplary implementation of systemic mentoring. It is a needed tool for follow-up and for writing substantive letters of recommendation.

The guidance to graduate school essentially begins the freshman year. The mere knowledge that most graduate schools require a 3.0/4.0 Grade Point Average (GPA) or higher is important for those who have any intentions of going for the Bachelor degree. Incidentally, most high tech firms, corporations or industries tend to require GPAs of 3.0/4.0 for their perspective summer interns or full-time employees. We underscore to the incoming classes the importance of graduate admission tests, from the Graduate Record Examination (GRE) and the Law School Admissions Test (LSAT) to the Graduate Management Admission Test (GMAT), and others. The various mechanisms for funding graduate studies, i.e., fellowships, scholarships, teaching assistantships, and research assistantships, are expounded upon for the freshman to grasp the various processes for acquiring funding for graduate studies. Good communication skills and research experiences are known to be competitive edges for graduate applicants. In addition to extensive research on the Web, exhibits of graduate schools at graduate fairs and at conferences are procedures for securing admission into a graduate school. Scholars who are to pursue graduate degrees are required to prepare and submit applications to at least three distinct graduate programs. These applications often include that for a graduate assistantship. LS-AMP alumni across the country have the opportunity to enroll in Bridge to the Doctorate (BD) activities on various campuses around the country. Our scholars are reminded of the above issues related to graduate studies from their freshman year to graduation. LS-LAMP and other mentoring units, like the D. M. R. Spikes Honors College, are in partnership with the Office of Career Services at SUBR. At least twice a year, over a two-day period (Saturday and Sunday), this office offers extensive professional development opportunities on career-related topics. Dining and etiquette, interview preparation, resume' writing, attire, credit and banking, and networking are among the specific topics explicitly addressed during these sessions. The above preparations for job seekers are useful even for the students who pursue Ph.D. degrees. From 2000 to 2012, **no less than 1031 scholars have benefited from this guidance to graduate school or to the job market.**

From 2000 to 2012, **30 former scholars received the Ph.D.** These students were all awarded STEM BS degrees from SUBR. These graduates have attained lucrative positions in industry, as post-doctoral fellows at research laboratories and at universities, and as professors in academia. **To date, four have had the highly competitive and substantial National Science Foundation's Graduate Research Fellowship.**

The significance of the approach and impact of LS-LAMP and the Timbuktu Academy stems from literally placing the creation of educational, research, and professional value-added (i.e., production of highly competitive graduates) on a rigorous scientific basis. **Representative teaching, mentoring, and learning (TML)**

articles are in the list of cited publications. More importantly, however, the Ten-Strand Systemic Mentoring model guarantees this integration. As such, LS-LAMP and the Timbuktu Academy constitute national treasures as attested to by the US Presidential awards for excellence in 2002 for the Academy and in 1996 for its director.

International Research Collaborations

Our scholars have traveled abroad to engage in international research programs. Specifically, two former scholars and graduates of SUBR, were selected to participate in two distinct summer research internships in Geneva, Switzerland. In the summers of 2001 and 2004, Marx Mbonye, Ph.D. student, and Dr. Divine Kumah, respectively, conducted research at CERN, the European Organization for Nuclear Research. These students were part of an international research collaboration which performs the ATLAS experiment at the Large Hadron Collider, the most powerful and largest particle accelerator in the world.

In the summer of 2010, two former scholars and Ph.D. students, Justin Boone and Frank Alexander Jr., participated in the 2010 NSF International Research and Education in Engineering Program to conduct engineering-related research in **Shanghai, China,** June - August 2010. Mr. Boone's research topic was "Inverter Efficiency in a Solar Powered Dehumidifier System." He monitored the behavior of efficiency versus output power of the system. Mr. Alexander served as an MRI researcher/assistant at Time-Medical Systems, working independently to simulate and test a spinal MRI coil design for MRI imaging.

From May 28 to June 2, 2010, two undergraduate scholars, Polite Stewart Jr. and Robert Florida Jr., and one former scholar and Ph.D. student, Phillip Jones, traveled to **Erice, Italy,** to partake in a course on the production and storage of renewable and sustainable energy. These students were participants in the Materials for Renewable Energy Conference at the International School of Solid State Physics. This event served as a mechanism to bring together young scientists and experts to share new knowledge and ideas on renewable energy.

In the summer of 2012, five scholars--Brianna Precciely, Krystal Finley, Shannon Jones-Butts, Melvin Watson-Richardson, and Donavon Walker--were accepted to study abroad for four weeks at Guizhou University in **Guiyang, China,** through the SUBR Office of Research and Strategic Initiatives and the Southern University's Global Sustainability Initiatives. This program afforded these scholars the opportunity to experience Chinese cultural activities and to participate in sustainable science field experiences including an ecosystem study at Huangguoshu PuBu Waterfall and Tianxing Qiao Natural Park. While participating in the program, these scholars were enrolled in two courses, Chinese Language and an Introduction to Sustainability, at Guizhou University.

References

1. Boff, K. R., Kaufman, L., and Thomas, J. P. (I986). Handbook of Perception and Human Performance, Vol. II, Cognitive Processes and Performance, John Wiley and Sons, San Francisco, Pages 28-71.
2. Snoddy, G.S. (1926), "Learning and Stability," Journal of Applied Psychology, 10, 1-36.
3. Newel, A. and Rosenbloom, P. S. Rosenbloom (1981). *Mechanisms of Skill Acquisition,* edited by Anderson, J. R. Hillsdale, NJ., USA: Erlbaum.
4. Bagayoko, D. and Kelley, E. L. (1994), "The Dynamics of Student Retention: A Review and a Prescription," Education, Vol. 115, No.1, 31-39.

5. Bagayoko, D., Hasan, S., and Kelley, E. L. (2000) "A Problem-Solving Paradigm." The Journal of College Teaching, Vol. 48 (1): 24-27.

BEST PRACTICES IN SYSTEMIC STEM MENTORING AT SOUTHERN UNIVERSITY AT NEW ORLEANS

Joe Omojola, Ph.D.

Southern University at New Orleans is a historically Black university and a long standing senior state institution in Louisiana which was founded as a branch of Southern University Agricultural and Mechanical College of Baton Rouge in 1959. The mission of SUNO is "to create and maintain an environment conducive to learning and growth, to promote the upward mobility of all people by preparing them to enter into new as well as traditional careers and to equip them to function optimally in the mainstream of the American society." SUNO is accredited by the Southern Association of Colleges and Schools and National

Council for Accreditation of Teacher Education. The institution was established primarily, but not exclusively, for the higher education of underrepresented minority citizens in the greater New Orleans area and the State of Louisiana. For the past two years, the average enrollment at SUNO has been 3,200 students with approximately 98% being underrepresented minority.

Expand Financial Support to Students

Funding for Scholarships for Excellence in Natural Sciences (SENS), a five-year, $600,000 program supports undergraduate students. Funding for Enhancement, Enrichment, and Excellence in Mathematics and Science (E3MaS), a five-year, $1.75 million NSF program to improve the quality of incoming high school students through Summer Enrichment Program, develop high school mathematics and science teachers through content enhancement workshops. E3MaS improves the academic quality of undergraduate students through scholarships, learning center support, research mentoring, placement in summer internships and GRE preparation. LS-LAMP's funds were used to support twenty-five STEM majors through scholarships, book stipends, travels, research incentives, and tuition. Thirty-two other students benefited from E3MaS and SENS funds.

Communication Skill Enhancement

The technical writing course and the advanced composition course are mandatory for science, technology, engineering, and mathematics (STEM) majors at SUNO. Additional resources were provided to STEM students through English instructors and the writing lab facilitated by the English Department. The writing lab was used to provide tutoring and editorial revisions for STEM majors. LS-LAMP students made presentations during the SUNO Undergraduate Research Day, and at national and regional conferences. Additionally, LS-LAMP students made presentations during LS-LAMP meetings on campus, and MathFest. Selected students in LS-LAMP made presentations at recruitment events organized by the College of Arts and Sciences.

Comprehensive, Scientific Advisement

SUNO LS-LAMP departmental mentoring coordinators are: Murty Kambhampati, Ph.D., biology; Carl Johnson, Ph.D., chemistry; and Joe Omojola, Ph.D., mathematics and physics. Mentors were recruited through announcements at College of Arts and sciences meetings, departmental meetings, and through interpersonal communications by campus and departmental mentoring coordinators. Documented contacts with LS-LAMP scholars are made during LS-LAMP seminars and meetings, mentoring sessions, tutoring sessions, and e-mails. Each STEM undergraduate student is assigned to a faculty advisor who is responsible for helping them plan and implement their degree programs sequentially.

At the beginning of each semester, proper training and workshops on advisement and related topics are conducted by the SUNO administration. Each faculty member is required to attend these trainings. SUNO continues to provide this service to all faculty members and staff. Relevant information on advisement and mentoring such as The Timbuktu Academy at www.phys.subr.edu/timbuktu.htm will continue to be disseminated among faculty members. The LS-LAMP coordinator maintains communication with other LS-LAMP coordinators through e-mails, telephone, and meetings to share relevant information on advisement and other matters.

Tutoring

Capable, upper level LS-LAMP students served as tutors in all STEM fields on campus. Some LS-LAMP students have also been enlisted to tutor introductory classes. In addition to strengthening the student tutors' skills, certificates and stipends were used as incentives for participation. Departmental coordinators facilitate tutoring for classes offered in their respective departments. In Fall 2011 semester, two faculty members and, in spring 2012, three mathematics faculty members agreed to provide tutoring in algebra, especially in critical areas that are essential to succeed in STEM courses. Arrangements were made for these faculty members to provide fifteen hours a week in the learning center. Some STEM software (MathLab, Octave, R software, GRE software, etc.) have been installed on the computers in the learning center.

Peer group tutoring is available in general chemistry, general physics, introductory biology, college algebra, and the calculus series. Group assignments are already in progress in every STEM discipline on campus. SUNO LS-LAMP continues to encourage and support these efforts. SUNO LS-LAMP encourages peer mentoring through referring students to specific student mentors in their major department. Student mentors assist in encouraging and tutoring underclassmen. This method has worked very well in the past. We will continue to use this method. SUNO LS-LAMP collaborates with the E3MaS program to provide textbooks and software in mathematics, physics, chemistry, and biology.

To extend this service, LS-LAMP will continue to purchase frequently used texts in STEM fields to facilitate students' learning. Because of our extremely large population of non-traditional (older, married (or single) with children, and working full time) students, we take advantage of distance learning. We also use soft-

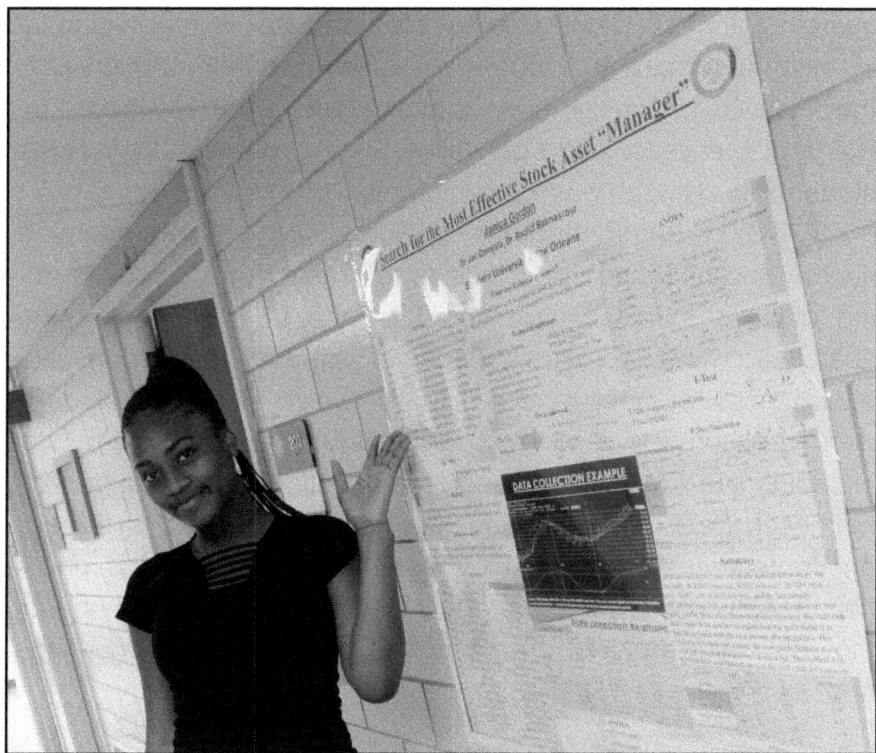

ware in our Math and Science Learning Center for students to take advantage of computer-aided tutoring. Presently, evening classes are scheduled to improve STEM retention among non-traditional students. Group study and peer interactions are encouraged among all students. We continue to reach out to more students by introducing faculty mentors to students during our seminars.

Introducing Students to Research Tools and Methods

LS-LAMP students are assigned to faculty mentors that work with them on undergraduate research. With the synergy produced with the E3MaS and SENS programs, we are increasing the number of undergraduate students that participate in research. SUNO LS-LAMP also assisted students with participating in external programs (such as Tulane LS-LAMP, University of Iowa, Xavier University, Penn State University, University of Louisiana at Lafayette, and Fort Valley State University) that mentor students in research during the summer months.

SUNO LS-LAMP students participate in undergraduate research and have the opportunities to present their research during campus seminars sponsored by the LS-LAMP office. Research activities were rewarded with stipends and sponsoring attendances at conferences. Up to twelve LS-LAMP students were sponsored to present at regional and national conferences including the Emerging Researchers' National Conference, and MathFest. Conference attendees were required to write a report on conferences in which they participated. Information on research activities are distributed to students and faculty members through notice boards, on the SUNO website, during meetings, and via e-mail.

Involving LS-LAMP Students in Hands-on Research

One of the requirements of SUNO LS-LAMP is participation in undergraduate research. As we continue to emphasize this, more faculty members and students are getting involved. Through our collaborations with other LS-LAMP institutions including Tulane University and Louisiana State University, more opportunities are made available to our students. SUNO LS-LAMP has successfully placed students at summer internships at Tulane University, Penn State University, Fort Valley State University, University of Alabama, University of Iowa, Auburn University, Dowling College, Rensselaer Polytechnic Institute, and Brookhaven National Lab (BNL).

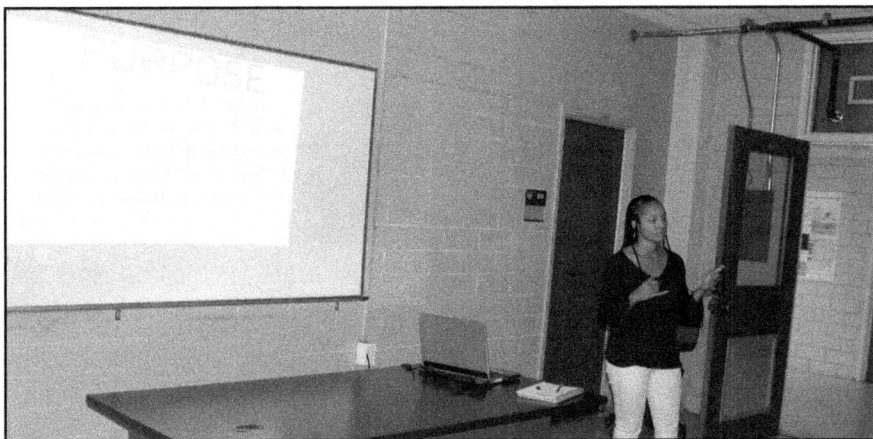

We will continue to engage students in these activities. Faculty participating in E3MaS has encouraged the program scholars to apply to 2011 summer undergraduate internships at national laboratories, research institutions and universities. Nineteen STEM students were placed in internships, out of the nineteen; eleven were placed in HBCU-UP at SUNO, two at BNL's FaST program, one at BNL's SULI program, three at SUNO – Oil Spill program, one at Penn State University and one at University of Louisiana at Lafayette. Fourteen of the students did their research in biology, four in mathematics, and one in chemistry.

Strengthen Professional Skills

SUNO LS-LAMP sponsored the following student clubs: biology club, mathematics club, BKX, NIS, and the National Association of Mathematicians. Student participation in professional conferences and meetings continues to be emphasized. In the past years our students have participated in MGE@MSA, ERN, and National Association of Mathematicians Regional conferences. Students also attended campus seminars. Faculty mentors work with LS-LAMP students to produce competitive research to be presented at local, state, regional, or national conference. LS-LAMP's funding helps to pay for preparation, travel, and accommodations for participants and faculty mentors. STEM majors participate in College Day, Graduate and professional Day and Undergraduate Research Day.

During these "days," students get acquainted with the campus, are exposed to opportunities in graduate programs and are given the opportunity to present their research. Guest speakers were also invited to SUNO campus to present. Noel Blackburn, FaST Program Manager at Brookhaven National Laboratory, visited SUNO in 2011. During his visit, Blackburn conducted a summative evaluation of the program, presented a seminar on opportunities available for STEM students and a presentation on chemical and environmental engineering to students enrolled in our Environmental Awareness class.

Jennifer Higbie, GIS Specialist at BNL, visited SUNO on March 27-28, 2012. During her visit, Higbie met with the E3MaS director and program managers to discuss the progress of the E3MaS program. She also met with STEM students and faculty and provided them with information about available research opportunities for students and faculty at BNL during the summer and academic year. In addition, she lectured and provided a hands-on laboratory activity during our Environmental Biotechnology class. Patrick Barnes, an environmental consultant, visited SUNO on April 11, 2012. During his visit, Barnes met with STEM faculty and students to discuss unique opportunities in environmental sciences in the aftermath of Hurricane Katrina. He also conducted an open discussion with STEM majors and faculty about expanding opportunities in the environmental science industry.

Development of Computer and Technological Skills

Applications for LS-LAMP and other scholarships have been redesigned so that applications can be completed online. This is done primarily to build and enhance computer skills while improving efficiency of the application process. In conjunction with mentors, student resumes are required by the LS-LAMP office in hardcopy and as an electronic file format. Students are also asked to write personal statements. The purpose of the personal statement is to help students hone their writing skills and maintain a written record of their goals. Students are also encouraged to prepare a personal statement for graduate school applications. STEM majors are encouraged to take classes in computer information systems to satisfy or exceed the State requirements for computer literacy. Students are also encouraged to take a programming class in cases where such classes are not mandated.

Monitor Student Performance

Faculty mentors were asked to maintain a log or record of their mentoring activities. The fact that these logs or records could be used as supporting documents for retention, tenure or promotion was used as an incentive. Scientific advisement, in which advisement of students was done objectively in accordance with a well-planned timeline, was encouraged by LS-LAMP. Monitoring of class attendance and performance of students are done by faculty mentors during meetings with their mentees. Advisement meetings between academic advisors and their students are mandated by each unit of the University. SUNO LS-LAMP supports the establishment of a tutoring lab where faculty members and selected, competent STEM students tutor a variety of science and mathematics courses. SUNO LS-LAMP maintains a database of current students' e-mails. The e-mails are used to communicate with students to inform them of available opportunities and to notify them of meetings, seminars, and other events.

Guidance to Graduate School

Prior to Hurricane Katrina, SUNO's GAELA program funded a GRE class attended by LS-LAMP students. GAELA funds were also used to pay for students who took the GRE after successfully completing the class. A new emphasis has been placed on purchasing GRE software for students' use. SUNO sponsors Graduate and Professional Day once each semester. This gives several universities the opportunity to visit SUNO and recruit students for graduate and professional schools. LS-LAMP will continue to support this activity. LS-LAMP and E3MaS also provide funding for students to visit neighboring universities who are recruiting for graduate STEM departments. SUNO LS-LAMP has always supported students in graduate school applications.

Specifically, our faculty mentors write many letters of recommendation for graduate and professional school applicants. Faculty mentors also aid in the preparation of personal statements. We will continue our commitment to this process. In our seminars, we devote time to discussions about the benefits of a graduate education. We will also take advantage of the graduate school seminars sponsored by LS-LAMP; SUNO (through the E3MaS program) has collaborations in place with Tulane University, Louisiana State University, University of Iowa, University of Mississippi, University of Alabama, Arizona State University, Xavier University, Dillard University, and Southern University at Baton Rouge. Other collaborations currently in place include University of New Orleans, University of Missouri, and University of Louisiana, Lafayette. We will continue to build on these collaborations and seek to expand them as opportunities arise.

Conference Participation

STEM faculty members, LS-LAMP, and E3MaS Scholars made presentations at the following national conferences:

- Five students and one faculty attended the Fifth Annual Mathematics Field of Dreams Conference at Arizona State University, Tempe AZ, (October 14-16, 2011);
- Eight students and two faculty members attended the LSU 3rd Annual Undergraduate Research (TRIPLE EX) Conference at Baton Rouge, LA. (November 4, 2011) -Tiaria Porche won first place in 1st Year Biology Researcher Category;

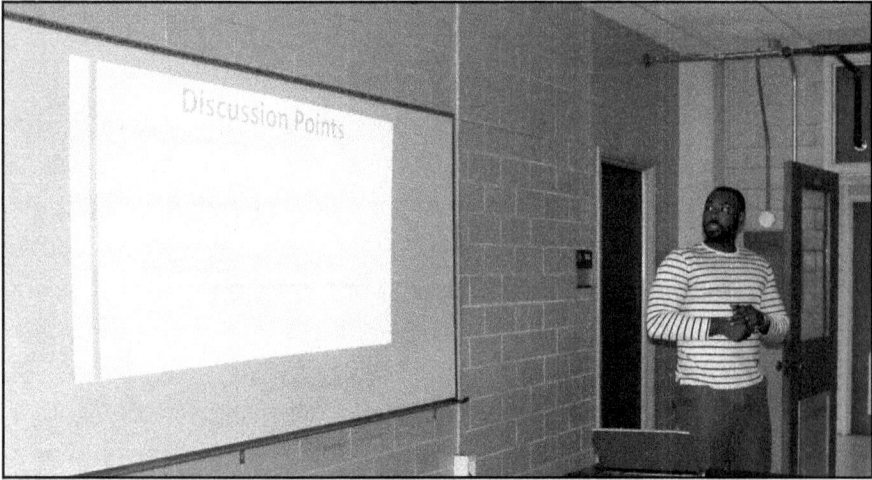

- Two students, one faculty member and a staff attended the National Association of Mathematicians MathFest XXI in New Orleans (November 3 -5, 2011);
- Seventeen students and 10 faculty members attended Southern University at New Orleans' Student Research Day (December 2, 2011);
- Five students attended the More Graduate Education at Mountain States Alliance MGE@MSA Conference, Arizona State University (February 13 – 14, 2012). Van Vu and Jasmine Jenkins each won second place in the poster presentations. Dot'Toya Jones and Aurellia Whitmore each received honorable mention certificates; and
- Eleven students and two faculty members attended Emerging Researchers National Conference in STEM in Atlanta, GA (February 23-25, 2012) – Gino Loverde won first place in mathematics oral presentation category.

Between March 21-25, 2012, 10 SUNO students – seven biology majors and three mathematics majors: Jasmin Jenkins, Monicah Jepkemboi, Dot'Toya Jones, Gawain Kiffin, Gino Loverde,

Tiaria Porche, Rispah Sang, Rickea Selmon, Van Vu, and Aurellia Whitemore attended the 69th Join Annual Meeting of BKX/NIS, held in Nashville, TN. The students were accompanied by Johnson, Kambhampati, and Omojola. During the conference, students presented their research, attended sessions on how to apply and pay for graduate school, and discussed disparities experienced by minority populations relating to health care. Faculty members volunteered their time to judge students' oral and postal presentations.

In the exhibition hall, students were able to visit graduate school recruiters from a range of universities around the country. During luncheons and dinners, several speakers presented. Most significantly, LaVeist spoke about how health disparities and access to care is impacted by socio-economic status. Five students won awards: Jasmin Jenkins (3rd place), Gawain Kiffin (3rd place), Gino Loverde (3rd place), Tiaria Porche (3rd place), and Aurellia Whitmore (3rd place).

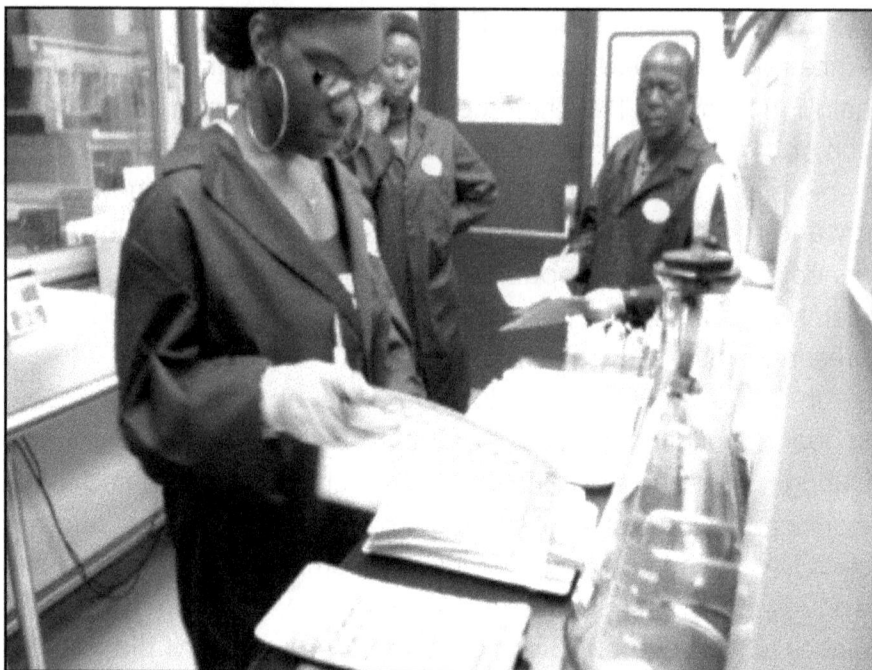

BEST PRACTICES IN SYSTEMIC STEM MENTORING AT SOUTHERN UNIVERSITY AT SHREVEPORT

Josephine P. Loston

The Louis Stokes - Louisiana Alliance for Minority Participation Program is designed to strengthen science, technology, engineering, and mathematics (STEM)teaching and research strategies; improve the access and retention of undergraduate students; prepare students academically and enhances professional skills by making the as competitive as possible for graduate school. SULA package, was initiated to enhance the quality of

STEM programs and impact STEM students throughout their education at Southern University at Shreveport Louisiana.

Accomplishments

The majority of SUSLA LS-LAMP participants are first-generation college students from economically disadvantaged communities who have been inspired by the possibility of obtaining an education. A vital part of the SUSLA LS-LAMP program is to increase the number of transferring students in scientific fields at four-year colleges or universities. In order to successfully fulfill the objectives of this program, the following work plan and subsequent objectives have been observed. The basis of addressing this objective lies in the creation of innovative techniques to stimulate the interest of students and to ensure that those students are prepared to meet those challenges by providing comprehensive preparation in a strong scientific background.

Several faculty members with firm research knowledge and experiences actively play a role in the science, technology, engineering, and mathematics LS-LAMP Program at SUSLA. The LS-LAMP Program at SUSLA has created an environment in which both students and faculty are continuously learning. The program has been committed to supporting and maintaining a team of well-qualified faculty for improving the quality of STEM education for SUSLA students. A number of SUSLA STEM faculty members, having firm research knowledge and expertise, actively participated in the LS-LAMP Program during the academic year and summer sessions. Faculty from these departments played a vital role in helping the students build an academic foundation for success and acquiring four-year degree readiness in STEM disciplines.

Students were actively engaged in research training throughout the academic year under the direct guidance of a faculty mentor. The faculty was also involved in the evaluation of STEM curriculum revision and enhancement to better prepare students with an academic foundation to excel in future STEM degree courses. The faculty continues to provide support to the LS-LAMP Program's administrative staff in the planning and implementation of structured academic year activities and events sponsored through the LS-LAMP Program.

The Research Infrastructure in Minority Institutions (RIMI) Program has improved the research infrastructure for students and professors. Students in the LS-LAMP Program are now able to observe and participate in research conducted by STEM faculty. Both programs are in the Division of Science and Technology, and are funded by the National Institutes of Health, Board of Regents and the National Science Foundation. The LS-LAMP, Historically Black College and University for Undergraduate Program (HBCU-UP), and RIMI Programs also worked together in coordinating scientific seminar series, pre-professional and professional development workshop activities for STEM students and faculty. The LS-LAMP Program continues to maintain a strong collaboration with HBCU-UP, which has significantly increased the transition of minority students from SUSLA's undergraduate STEM programs to any college/university in Louisiana in pursuit of a STEM baccalaureate degree.

Our goals are to expose LS-LAMP students to career opportunities in STEM and to strengthen STEM students' research strategies in order to improve access and retention of undergraduates in the STEM disciplines. Another goal is to prepare undergraduate students academically so as to enhance their scientific and professional competitiveness as the students pursue STEM disciplines at the graduate level at other universities. Since the inception of the program, motivated freshman and sophomore students and faculty members have broadened their research

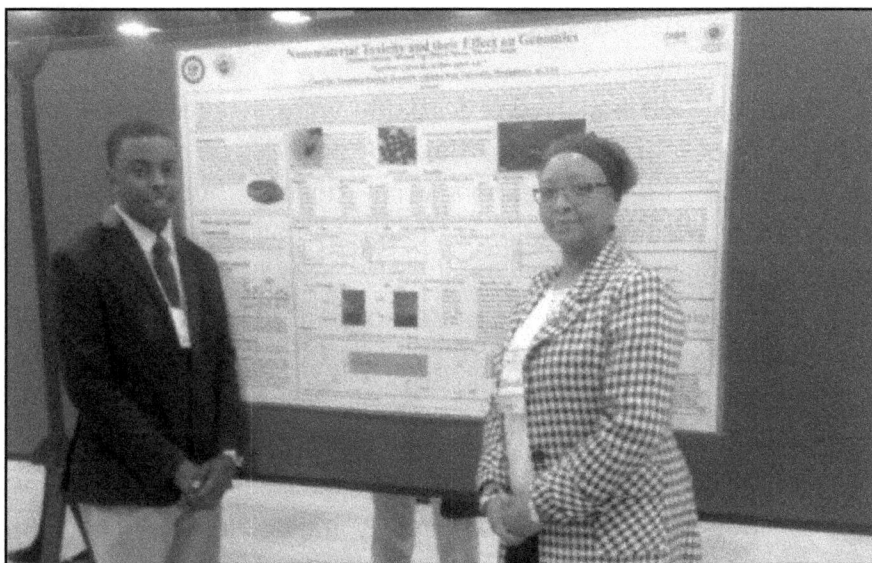

knowledge and training through support from the LS-LAMP Program and external research academic institutions and industries.

During the academic year, our STEM students are involved in research. Their research activities are limited due to their academic class work. During the summer, they are provided the opportunity to participate in an eight-week to ten-week summer research undergraduate program. They are engaged in cutting edge, hands-on research, which allows them the opportunity to enhance their basic lab and computer skills, with the assistance of an established research scientist. The students also have the opportunity of being exposed to their peers giving seminars, presenting posters, and interacting with students from similar backgrounds. Faculty members spend time providing basic hands-on research trainings on different instruments to be used during the proposed project. Also, faculty members encourage students to prepare and help them to participate in presenting scientific seminars. A total of forty-two STEM faculty and students presented scientific seminars to STEM faculty and students during the fall and spring semesters.

More than 60 faculty and students were in attendance each week. For each participant, faculty provide several possible projects, concepts for experimental design, hypothesis, and analyses of results to students for presentation at national and regional meetings.

- Lonnie McCray, Ph.D., professor of English, Southern University at Shreveport, LA, "Writing Personal Statements" (2014)
- Kirk Grain, Ph.D., professor of biology, Southern University at Shreveport, LA "Research at a Glance" (2014)
- Shirley M. Roberson, director of multicultural affairs, Louisiana State University Health Sciences Center-Shreveport - "Partnerships in Science Pipelines Recruitment and Retention" (2014)
- Ashley Fitzgerald, Ph.D., biology professor, Southern University at Shreveport, LA "Characterization and Function of Follistatin in Human Trabecular Mechwork Cells and Tissues," (SUSLA), (2014)
- Ratonya Bennett, Southern University at Shreveport, LA "Test Taking Skills" (2014)
- Charles Newton, computer science major, Southern University at Shreveport, LA "Calculating DNA Binding Sites" (2014)
- Jeremy Taylor, biology major, Southern University at Shreveport, LA "Tap Water vs. Bottled Water" (2014)
- Debra Williams, computer science major, Southern University at Shreveport, LA "Autism" (2014)

- Naidu Seetala, Ph.D., physics professor, Grambling State University, Grambling, LA "Summer Research at Grambling" (2014)
- Gwendolyn Tennell, computer science major, Southern University at Shreveport, LA "A Tutorial of the Caliope2SP Functioning Simply with Robotic Operating System" (2014)
- Chelsea Roberson , biology major, Southern University at Shreveport, LA "Cervical Cancer" (2014)
- D'Anthoni Woodard, computer science major, Southern University at Shreveport, LA "Coliform in Cross Lake Water Shed"(2014)
- Makram A. Himaya, Ph.D., professor, Grambling State University, Grambling, LA "ABRCMS" (2014)
- Emmanuel Clottey, Ph.D., Louisiana State University at Shreveport "Careers in Kinesiology and Public Health" (2014)
- John Bell, computer science major, Southern University at Shreveport, LA "Interactive Chromatin Modeling program" (2014)
- Tashonda Benoit, biology major, Southern University at Shreveport, LA "E - COLI" (2014)
- Joseph Corpprue, biology major, Southern University at Shreveport, LA "Spinal Cord Injuries" (2014)
- Michael County, chemistry major, Southern University at Shreveport, LA "Processed Foods" (2014)
- Treasure Dotson, engineering major, Southern University at Shreveport, LA "Nanotechnology Toxicity and Their Effect on Genomics" (2014)
- Keldric Jones, biology major, Southern University at Shreveport, LA "A Needs Assessment Study for Establishing a Certified Primary Stroke Center" (2014)

- Wiley College Business Department – Financial Literacy Organization"Money Management Matters" – Marshall, TX (2014)
- Aterica Pearson, biology major, Southern University at Shreveport, LA "Chlamydia Major Outer Membrane Protein" (2014)
- Jakhobi McDaniel, biology major, Southern University at Shreveport, LA "Affects of Alhimia" (2014)
- Breanna Manning, biology major, Southern University at Shreveport, LA "COBOL vs. JAVA Computer Language" (2014)
- Emmanuel Sims, engineering major, Southern University at Shreveport, LA "College Students' Perceptions about a Stroke" (2014)
- Justina Eneche, biology major, Southern University at Shreveport, LA "Microglia Activation in Wild Type Mice and Transgenic Mice" (2014)
- Stanley Sandifer, mathematics major, Southern University at Shreveport, LA "What Happens to the Immunization Cells during Asthma?" (2014)
- Dyamond Williams, computer science major, Southern University at Shreveport, LA "Effect of Firing Time on YSZ Microstructure for NOx Sensing" (2014)
- Lonnie McCray, Ph.D, professor of English, Southern University at Shreveport, "Writing Personal Statements" (2015)
- Ratonya Bennett, counselor, Southern University at Shreveport, LA "Test Taking Skills" (2015)
- Makram A. Himaya, Ph.D., professor, Grambling State University, Grambling, LA "MARC NIH Program" (2015)
- Jakhobi McDaniel, biology major, Southern University at Shreveport, LA "Pox Virus" (2015)

- Treasure Dotson, electronics technology major, Southern University at Shreveport, LA "Nanotechnology Toxicity and Their Effect on Genomics" (2015)
- Joseph Cropprue, biology major, Southern University at Shreveport, LA "Practices and Procedures of a Physical Therapist" (2015)
- Keldric Jones, biology major, Southern University at Shreveport, LA "A Needs Assessment Study for Establishing a Certified Primary Stroke Center" (2015)
- La'Briquois Wilson, Captain Shreve High School, Shreveport, LA, "Test How the Number of Letters (or Characters) in a File Change the Size of the File" (2015)
- Clara Tobin, Airline High School, Shreveport, LA "Synthesis of Phthalocyanines" (2015)
- Levi Brown, Evangel Christian Academy, Shreveport, LA "Converting Waste Food into a Useful Resource" (2015)
- Jasqueline Staton, Fair Park High School, Shreveport, LA "Detection of Coliform Bacteria from Various Water Sources and Inanimate Objects " (2015)
- Angelica Tobin, Airline High School, Shreveport, LA "Phthalocyamines" (2015)
- Joseph I. Orban, Ph.D., dean, science and liberal arts, Southern University at Shreveport, LA "Poultry Production in Space: Fantasy or Reality" (2015)
- Naidu Seetala, Ph.D., physics professor, Grambling State University, Grambling, LA "Summer Research at Grambling," (2015)

Meetings and Conferences

To broaden students' scientific writing and speaking abilities, LS-LAMP and HBCU-UP strongly support student participation in scientific meetings and conferences. In this effort, several SUSLA

STEM scholars participated in the following local, regional, and national scientific meetings and conferences:

- Eighteen STEM scholars attended the 2013 South Central Chapter of Society of Toxicology Annual Fall Meeting in Baton Rouge, LA. The STEM scholars were John Bell – presented research - (computer science), Michael County – presented research (chemistry), Treasure Dotson (Electronics Technology), Jakhobi McDaniel - (biology), Charles Newton – presented research - (computer science), Aterica Pearson – presented research (biology), Emmanuel Sims – presented research (electronics technology), Johan Von-Behr – presented research (chemistry), Dyamond Williams – presented research - (computer science), Benjamin Siele (biology), Justina Eneche (biology), Joseph Cropprue (biology), Tashonda Benoit (biology), Keldric Jones (biology), Debra Williams (computer science), Richard Williams (electronics technology), D'Anthoni Woodard (biology), and Stanley Sandifer (mathematics).
- Nine STEM scholars attended the 2013 NANOBIO Summit in Montgomery, AL. The STEM scholars were Dyamond Williams, (computer science) – presented research, Gwendolyn Tennell, (computer science) – presented research, Aterica Pearson (biology) – presented research, Jakhobi McDaniel, (biology), Charles Newton, (computer science) – presented research, Michael County, (chemistry) – presented research, Emmanuel Sims (electronics technology) – presented research, Keldric Jones (biology), and Johan VonBehr, (chemistry) – presented research.
- Fourteen STEM scholars attended the Louis Stokes Midwest Center of Excellence Conference in Indianapolis, IN. The STEM scholars were Aterica Pearson, (biology) – presented

research, Charles Newton, (computer science) – presented research, Chelsea Roberson, (biology), D'Anthoni Woodard, (biology), Darrin Johnson, (biology), Debra Williams, (computer science), Dyamond Williams, (computer science) – presented research, Emmanuel Sims, (electronics technology) – presented research, Johan VonBehr (chemistry) – presented research, John Bell, (computer science) – presented research, Justina Eneche, (biology), Keldric Jones, (biology), Michael County, (chemistry) – presented research, and Treasure Dotson, (electronics technology).

- Nineteen STEM scholars attended the Annual Biomedical Conference for Minority Students (ABRCMS) in Nashville, TN. They were John Bell, (computer science) – presented research, Tashonda Benoit, (biology), Brandon Brooks, (biology), Michael County, (chemistry) – presented research, Joseph Cropprue, (biology), Treasure Dotson, (electronics technology), Beniesha Manning, (biology), Jakhobi McDaniel, (biology), Charles Newton, (computer science), – presented research, Aterica Pearson, (biology), – presented research, Chelsea Roberson, (biology), Stanley Sandifer (mathematics), Emmanuel Sims, (electronics technology) – presented research, Gwendolyn Tennell, (computer science) – presented research, Johan Von Behr, (chemistry) – presented research, Debra Williams (computer science), Dyamond Williams (computer science) – presented research, Richard Williams, (electronics technology), and D'Anthoni Woodard (biology).

- Three STEM scholars attended the American Association of Advancement of Science in Chicago, IL. The scholars were John Bell (computer science), Gwendolyn Tennell, (computer science) – presented research, and Dyamond Williams, (computer science) – presented research.

- Ten STEM scholars attended the Emerging Researchers National Conference in Washington, DC. They were John Bell (computer science), Terrence Arkansas (mathematics), Michael County (chemistry), Charles E. Newton (computer science), Aterica Pearson (biology), Gwendolyn Tennell (computer science), Chelsea Roberson (biology), Emmanuel Sims (electronics technology), Camille Tademy (biology), and Dyamond Williams (computer science).

- Seven STEM scholars attended the 2014 Xavier University Seventh Health Disparities Conference in New Orleans, LA. The STEM scholars were Michael County, (computer science) – presented research, Charles Newton, (computer science) - presented research, Chelsea Roberson, (biology), Joseph Orban, Ph.D., and D'Anthoni Woodard (biology), – presented research.

- Eighteen STEM scholars attended the 2014 American Chemical Society National Meeting in Dallas, TX. The STEM scholars were John Bell (computer science), Michael County, (chemistry), – presented research, Joseph Cropprue, (biology), Treasure Dotson (Electronics Technology), Keldric Jones, (biology), Beniesha Manning (biology), Jakhobi McDaniel, Charles Newton (computer science), Chelsea Roberson, (biology), Stanley Sandifer (mathematics), Emmanuel Sims, (electronics technology), Camille Tademy, (biology), Jeremy Taylor (electronics technology), Gwendolyn Tennell – presented research (computer science), Debra Williams (computer science), Dyamond Williams, (computer science), Brandon Brooks (biology), Justina Eneche, (biology).

- Eight STEM scholars attended the Grambling State University in Grambling, LA. The STEM scholars were Charles E. Newton (computer science), Aterica Pearson (biology), Gwendolyn Tennell (computer science), Chelsea Roberson (biology), Emmanuel Sims (electronics technology), Camille Tademy (biology), and Dyamond Williams (computer science) and John Bell (computer science).

Summer Undergraduate Research Exchange Program

This component of the program is designed to provide summer research opportunities for undergraduates interested in gaining experience in scientific research. Through this effort, eight students have gained successful entry into summer programs:

- Computer science scholar John Bell – Research topic: "Performance and Power Efficient Multi Core Computation"
- Biology scholar Joseph Cropprue - Research topic: "Practices and Procedures of a Physical Therapist"
- Electronics technology scholar Treasure Dotson – Research topic: "Nanotechnology Toxicity and Their Effect on Genomics"

- Biology scholar Justina Eneche – Research topic: "Microglia Activation in Wild Type Mice and Transgenic Mice"
- Biology scholar Keldric Jones – Research topic: "A Needs Assessment Study for Establishing a Certified Primary Stroke Center"
- Computer science scholar Charles Newton - Research topic: "Data and Analysis Semantics in Optical Sciences"
- Biology scholar Beniesha Manning – Research topic: "Aligning the Hinge of the External Fixator to the Elbow Using a Navigational SySTEM"
- Computer science scholar Gwendolyn Tennell – Research topic: "A Tutorial of the Caliope2SP Functioning Simply with Robotic Operating SySTEM"

Curriculum Reform Improvement

The gate-keeping courses in STEM disciplines have been revised by enhancing entry-level lab/research exercises in the present curriculum. This included updating equipment and teaching activities in existing laboratory classes in biology, chemistry, computer science, electronic technology, and mathematics. The revision of these courses include: evaluation and adaptation of additional/new textbooks; improvement in the methods of instructional delivery to include more short quizzes, inquiry-based learning, group assignments, tutorial sessions; and increased use of computer technology. Ongoing student tutorial assistance will be expanded to improve the performance of students in gate-keeping bottleneck STEM courses.

Peer Tutors

Select STEM scholars served as undergraduate peer tutors in the Tutorial Lab Center which is supported by the LS-LAMP and HBCU-UP programs. These programs provide tutoring and mentoring to qualified individuals. These joint efforts will continue throughout the implementation of the grant.

Five STEM scholars were selected based on their outstanding academic performance while serving as undergraduate peer tutors during the 2014 academic year: Emmanuel Sims – mathematics; Keldric Jones – biology; Charles Newton – computer science; Jennifer Sargent – mathematics and Daniel Ukpadi – chemistry. During the course of the program, peer tutors have become positive role models and have aided in recruiting new scholars into the STEM academic year program. Peer tutors are placed in the Division of Science and Technology Tutorial Lab.

Four-year University Transition: Acceptance Initiatives

LS-LAMP and HBCU-UP offer a variety of educational and enrichment activities designed to promote and create awareness, enhance students' competitiveness, and assist promising motivated students in admission to four-year schools. These activities include, but are not limited to, on-campus and off-site research training, inter-disciplinary guest speaker scientific seminars, educational tutorials, pre-professional development workshops, admission requirements, and financial aid process workshops.

Through the educational and enrichment activities at SUSLA, ten 2014 scholars graduated and were accepted into STEM programs at four-year universities.

- Computer science scholar John Bell, Louisiana State University at Shreveport, LA
- Chemistry scholar Michael County Jr., University of Houston at Houston, TX

- Biology scholar Beniesha Manning, Spelman College at Atlanta, GA
- Computer science scholar Charles Newton, Grambling State University, Grambling, LA
- Biology scholar Aterica Pearson, Grambling State University, Grambling, LA
- Mathematics scholar Stanley Sandifer, Louisiana State University at Shreveport, LA
- Electronic engineering scholar Emmanuel Sims, Jarvis Christian College, Hawkins, TX
- Computer science scholar Gwendolyn Tennell, Louisiana State University at Shreveport, LA
- Computer science scholar Debra Williams, Louisiana State University at Shreveport, LA
- Computer science scholar Dyamond Williams, Louisiana State University at Shreveport, LA

Outreach Activities

Listed below are the bridging strategies used to address high school/undergraduate, undergraduate/graduate, and university/job market transitions for underrepresented minorities in STEM fields.

In an effort to attract talented students to the STEM Program, application packets containing program brochures were widely distributed to college bound students during the annual "Senior Day" campus event. Application packets were also distributed to Ark-La-Tex high schools. More than 700 students visited the campus. To bring exposure to the LS-LAMP Program, recruitment specialists from the SUSLA Admissions and Recruitment Office continue to disseminate program flyers and applications to high school students throughout the parishes.

To bring exposure to the LS-LAMP Program, faculty and students visited area high schools twice a year to discuss the program with high school students and the academic and non-academic factors that are critical to success in college. The team also disseminated program flyers and applications to the high school students.

The LS-LAMP Program is featured at www.suslau.edu/lamp. The website presents opportunities offered by the program. To bring additional exposure to the LS-LAMP Program, brochures and promotional flyers are routinely distributed. Efforts for identifying and recruiting students are made through departmental tours. Activities are displayed on informational boards in the Louis Collier Building to make students aware of upcoming educational events and other STEM opportunities.

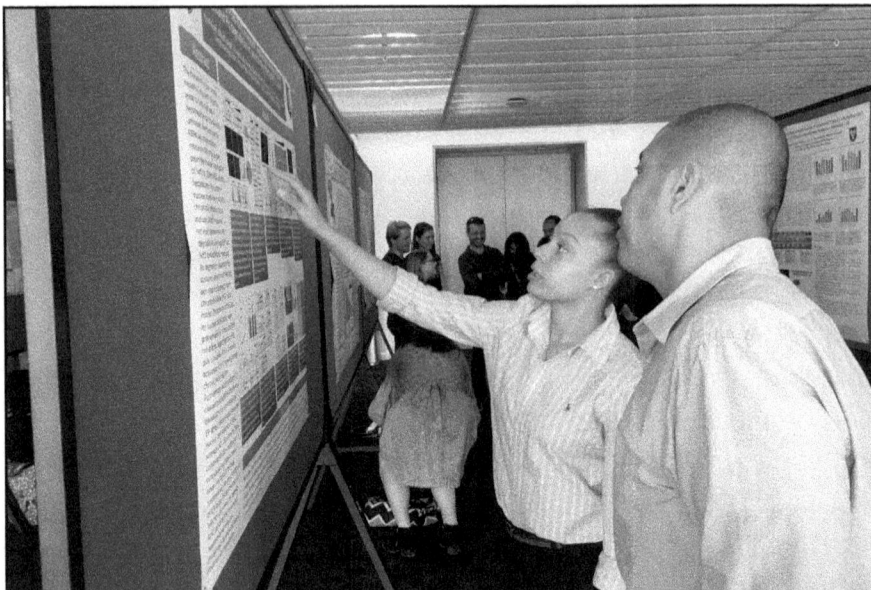

BEST PRACTICES IN SYSTEMIC STEM MENTORING AT TULANE UNIVERSITY

Michael Cunningham, Ph.D., and Eric Roque

As an institution ranked among the top fifty research universities in the nation, and one of the top graduate research universities in Louisiana, Tulane University is positioned to play an important role in meeting the statewide goals of LS-LAMP. Tulane University's primary role in the LS-LAMP program is to provide research opportunities to minority students. Providing undergraduate opportunities to participate in scientific research is an effective means of motivating them to pursue graduate education and, ultimately, careers in sciences. This is the rationale for many of the undergraduate research programs offered through granting agencies and institutions of higher learning. Likewise, research opportunities targeted at minority undergraduates is an effective means of recruiting minorities into the sciences.

Overall Goals and Objectives

The main goal of the LS-LAMP Program at Tulane is to increase the number and quality of underrepresented minority students enrolling in and completing baccalaureate degrees in science, technology, engineering and mathematics and subsequently pursuing graduate studies in STEM disciplines.

Systemic Mentoring Activities

For seventeen years, the Tulane LS-LAMP program has focused on offering research experiences for underrepresented minority undergraduates at Tulane. In 2010 LS-LAMP became part of the Research Engagement Core of Tulane's Center for Engaged Learning and Teaching (CELT). CELT was formed as a result of Tulane University's Quality Enhancement Plan to enhance student learning at Tulane. CELT's Research Engagement Core is focused on the common theme of "Purposeful Engagement in Learning." The union solidifies the university's commitment to making mentored, research, scholarship, and public creative expression an integral part of engaged learning at Tulane. Both CELT and LS-LAMP recognize the importance of undergraduate participation in research and the benefits of working with faculty, graduate students, and postdoctoral fellows. Furthermore, research opportunities help participants develop specialized knowledge of their major area of study, encourage research presentation, and develop their potential for graduate or professional school.

In 2010, the LS-LAMP Scholars Program was formed to increase the number of unrepresented minority STEM students participating in lab research at Tulane during the academic year. Each semester, six student researchers are selected from all STEM disciplines to work together on research projects with Tulane faculty mentors. Student learning objectives include and are not limited to the application of advanced research skills and activities, improvement of communication and presentation skills, increased intellectual curiosity, confidence, and motivation, clearer understanding of career interests, undergraduate retention and the increased likelihood to pursue graduate/advanced degrees. Faculty learning objectives include enhanced understanding of effective mentoring and the likelihood to continue to conduct research with the participation of minority STEM undergraduate students.

During the academic year, students participate in all facets of research, write a research paper, and/or present a poster on their research results at a national scientific conference. Each LS-LAMP Scholar receives a $3,000 stipend, along with a travel supplement to present their research, for their involvement in the program. Students are required to conduct research for the full semester. Faculty mentors are strongly encouraged to involve their mentees in these or other national or regional research conferences. We expect that the faculty mentor and student researcher partnership continues and possibly results in the publication of the student's contribution to the research project. Furthermore, the Tulane LS-LAMP Program provides limited financial support to help cover publication costs and costs associated with research lab materials.

Since Fall 2011, twenty-eight underrepresented minority students at Tulane have been placed in research positions with Tu-

lane Faculty during the academic school year. At least five students have gone on to present their research results at national scientific conferences and one student has been listed as a co-author in a research publication.

Additionally, the Tulane LS-LAMP Program works to involve Tulane faculty and currently enrolled Tulane STEM graduate and undergraduate students in activities designed to increase minority STEM retention, graduation and graduate school enrollment. Activities include seminars and workshops on study skills, peer mentoring, and communication skills, applying to graduate school, and research presentation skills. Students receive small scholarships for their involvement in these activities. In keeping in line with the focus on research engagement, seminars and workshops are scheduled throughout the academic year with topics on research goals clarification, securing research placements, selecting mentors, working with mentors, and issues of responsible research. Tulane research mentors (faculty, post-doctoral fellows, graduate students, and peer mentors) are encouraged participate in workshops and seminars on best practices and effective mentoring.

Conclusion

Using the research capabilities of Tulane faculty to enrich the quality of undergraduate experience and engaging students in research opportunities that complement their academic and career goals is a top priority of CELT and LS-LAMP. Tulane is committed to supporting the research enterprise, to improve the infrastructure, to eliminate institutional barriers to effective research and to reward success in research. As a result, the University strives to increase its levels of federal research and development funding, especially in the sciences and engineering. Furthermore, investments in environments supporting research positively impacts graduate education at Tulane. This commitment supports the institutionalization of LS-LAMP activities.

BEST PRACTICES IN SYSTEMIC STEM MENTORING AT THE UNIVERSITY OF LOUISIANA AT LAFAYETTE

Bobbie DeCuir, Ph.D.

The University of Louisiana at Lafayette, the largest member of the University of Louisiana System, is a public institution of higher education offering bachelors, masters, and doctoral degrees. Within the Carnegie classification, UL Lafayette is designated as a research university with high research activity. The University's academic programs are administered by the colleges of the arts, education, engineering, general studies, liberal arts, and nursing allied health professions, B. I. Moody III College of Business Administration, Ray P. Authement College of the Sciences, and the graduate school. The University is dedicated to achieving excellence in undergraduate and graduate education, in research, and in public service.

For undergraduate education, this commitment implies a fundamental subscription to general education, rooted in the primacy of the traditional liberal arts and sciences as the core around which all curricula are developed.

The graduate programs seek to develop scholars who will variously advance knowledge, cultivate aesthetic sensibility, and improve the material conditions of humankind. The University reaffirms its historic commitment to diversity and integration. Thus, through instruction, research, and service, the University promotes regional economic and cultural development, explores solutions to national and world issues, and advances its reputation among its peers.

ULL is located in Lafayette, a city of 125,000 situated in an area of south Louisiana known as Acadiana. Many of the inhabitants of Acadiana—the numerous parishes that encompass Lafayette—are descendants of African, French and Spanish settlers. Culturally, the region is characterized by a joie de vivre, or joy of life. Acadiana residents are known for working hard and playing hard. Fairs and festivals throughout the year celebrate everything from alligators to zydeco music. Lafayette's annual Festival International de Louisiane has showcased musicians from French-speaking countries from around the world.

The University of Louisiana at Lafayette has been ranked among the top 100 public research universities in the United States, based on external funding its faculty members have attracted. The University has integrated an enriching student experience with the intellectual energy and solution-focused capabilities of a research university. With the recent creation of an Office of Distance and Electronic Learning, UL Lafayette's evolution includes the addition of more online courses and online degree programs that expand students' learning opportunities beyond the traditional classroom.

Overall Goals sand Objectives

The LS-LAMP Program has been an integral part of the University's mission to assure that under-represented minority students are better represented in graduate education leading to STEM degree attainment. The LS-LAMP Program is designed to: increase the number and quality of minority students earning baccalaureate degrees in science, technology, engineering and mathematics; and increase proportionately the number of minority students enrolling and succeeding in STEM graduate programs.

The goals and objectives of the program are garnered through a holistic and comprehensive set of services based on the Ten-Strand Systemic Mentoring Model. Once institutionalized this model of services can for many academies be the answer to the retention and graduation of minority students at the undergraduate level, and at the graduate level. Systemic change is only achieved through the interlacing of a definitive set of multi-level initiatives, therefore it is extremely important to build a broad coalition of advocates for change at different levels of the academy if change is to be sustained over time. This success at UL Lafayette is partly due to the partnerships and collaborations that we have formed over the years, but more importantly our success is garnered through the adherence to the Ten-Strand Mentoring Model developed through the Timbuktu Academy at Southern University and A&M College. The purpose of this report is to provide data-driven information regarding the implementation of this model along with the goals and activities that are in place to ensure fidelity.

Financial Support

The LS-LAMP staff informs students of the financial resources available to them through seminars that are offered on a semester basis through participating in programs. These seminars are designed to help students find avenues for diversifying their financial aid portfolios.

A variety of opportunities exist on our campus to assist those students majoring in STEM disciplines and those students who have performed well in high school. LS-LAMP staff reviews each participant's financial aid award. Seminars conducted include:

1. The Most Important 24 Hours: Keeping TOPS: This seminar is designed to remind students of the requirements necessary for maintaining their TOPS scholarships.
2. Pell Grants: How to Maintain Aid Eligibility and the Number of semesters of eligibility.
3. Loans: Not All are Created Equally.
4. College Work Study: Is this a job for you?
5. Student Support Services STEM: Grant Aid for STEM Only Students.
6. LS-LAMP: Is a Ph.D. in Your Future?
7. Scholarships: Once You are Here...Offers are in Your College!
8. Financial Literacy

The current struggle to improve the degree attainment of minority and low-income students comes at a time of increased fiscal pressures for institutions of higher education. Given that state and federal appropriations for higher education have been drastically reduced over the past few years, institutions have compensated for the lack of increased government support by increasing tuition. This also has the effect of limiting access to those students who can afford to pay for college. These workshops are based on research and analyses of differences among racial groups with regard to student aid which indicates that minority students are less likely to persist if financial aid levels are not adequate (Kaltenbaugh, St. John, and Starkey, 1999).

Communication Skill Enhancement

Achieving academic success on a college campus is, in large part, predicated upon students' respective exposure to academic discourse and willingness to learn and employ it. By "academic discourse," we mean the specific yet tacit discursive style expected of participants in the academy. Although language, literacy, and identity are inextricably linked with culture, researchers on minority students' experiences in mainstream colleges and universities have not focused on how linguistic differences negatively affect minority students' success in college (Bunch, 2009).

Ignorance of and resistance to academic discourse result in far too many students remaining outsiders to and often dropouts from a powerful means to greater academic and personal success: the university. It is not surprising, then, that many minority students seem under prepared for college; they are unfamiliar with and sometimes unwilling to employ the linguistic "cultural capital" needed for success in higher education. (Ladson-Billings, 1995)

Therefore, the UL Lafayette LS-LAMP Program's Communication Prep activities highlight: (a) the central role that literacy, specifically academic literacy plays in collegiate success (and, with such success, a feeling of integration into the college community); and (b) the primary reasons that many minority students do not learn or employ this discourse. Every fall and spring semester, the LS-LAMP office prepares students who are enrolled in the program to meet with potential mentors. These activities aim to increase these students' ability to successfully navigate an interview set up by them with a potential mentor in their respective STEM discipline. The activities associated with these goals include:

1. The lectures "Academic Discourse" and "Why It's Important" are given at the beginning of the semester.

2. Students must then prepare to research their potential mentor in their discipline and must secure a date with the LS-LAMP program assistant to discuss the information that they find.

3. Students are then required to role-play with the LS-LAMP Staff in a scheduled LS-LAMP meeting. Students are given pointers from LS-LAMP staff and other LS-LAMP scholars.

4. Meetings are then set up with potential mentors and the results of those meetings are discussed with each participant individually.

5. LS-LAMP meetings also provide a venue for students to present the research that they are working on with their mentors.

6. LS-LAMP scholars and their mentors travel to STEM conferences where they present either papers or posters.

7. Collaborations with the McNair Program at UL Lafayette allow students to take part in workshops that are geared towards effective presentation and delivery styles.

Comprehensive, Scientific Advisement

Key to student success in college is the proper sequencing of courses through structured advising activities. The LS-LAMP staff serves in an informal capacity for its participants. Each semester participants are required to attend informal advising sessions.

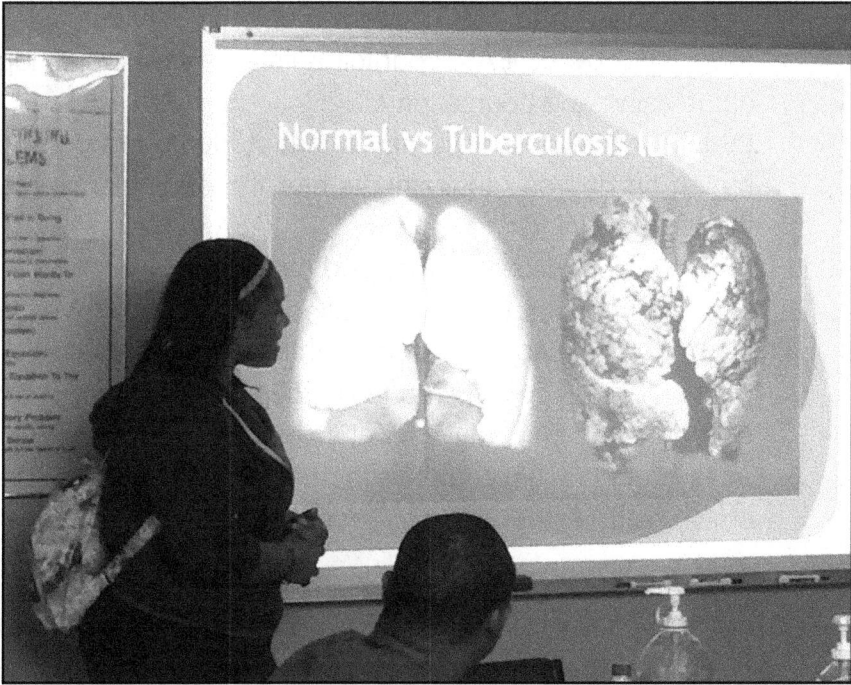

They are encouraged to register for appropriate classes in order to remain on schedule to complete coursework leading toward graduation. In addition, these discussions determine if there are any academic resources that the student might require and time management plans are developed tailored for each individual student. Activities associated with the fulfillment of this goal include:

1. Students are required to attend informal advising sessions with the LS-LAMP staff prior to university scheduled advising.
2. LS-LAMP staff have ongoing conversations with STEM chairs to garner support and keep abreast of any changes in the colleges.

3. Partnerships with the Student Support Services STEM Program allow LS-LAMP participants access to workshops on advising and course loads.
4. LS-LAMP staff check to insure that students are on track based on degree requirements and the particular catalog they are following.
5. Tentative schedules are mapped out.
6. Academic resources are discussed and planned for use in the upcoming semester along with tutoring schedules.
7. Students are then required to bring in a time management schedule once they have a set schedule.
8. After students have met with their formal advisor, they email the LS-LAMP office their set schedule.

Tutoring

The LS-LAMP Program strives to ensure that all students are given the full opportunity to discover and develop their talents, interests, and unique potential, and to provide a learning-centered and student-centered environment that presents the context for intellectual, and personal growth during college experiences. Each student learns to become independent, confident learners and develops good study habits and time management skills.

Many of our LS-LAMP participants serve as peer counselor tutors as they progress. LS-LAMP students are the first choice when hiring tutors for the Student Support Services-STEM lab. The activities that the LS-LAMP office provides to ensure that these goals are attained include:
1. Workshops addressing effective study group strategies;
2. Pairing upper level LS-LAMP scholars with freshmen students to assist them in acclimating to university culture;
3. Problem solving sessions through GRE preparation;

4. Utilization of computer software to enhance mathematics skills;

5. Exploration and implementation of alternative learning strategies through continued discussions with STEM faculty; and

6. LS-LAMP students enrolled in their first calculus class are paired with the mathematics specialist from the Student Support Services Program due to the collaborative efforts that are allowed for programs serving under represented students.

Generic Research Activities

Each Spring semester, the Black Faculty and Staff Association sponsors a research forum that invites faculty researchers from each college at the University. These researchers present their current research projects and allow time for questions and answers. LS-LAMP scholars are required to attend STEM related sessions. Exposure to these activities will present scholars with an opportunity to witness a research plan from conceptualization to completion. Other activities that forward this goal include:

1. Scholars are assigned to mentors who may utilize their services initially to complete literature reviews.

2. LS-LAMP staff collect and disseminate all summer research opportunities and post these on the LS-LAMP board and through email.

3. LAMP students are encouraged to apply to summer research internships.

4. Campus research experiences for undergraduate students are encouraged and sought out by the LS-LAMP office.

5. LS-LAMP scholars are required to write summaries of the IR research activities that they attend.

Specific Research Project Execution

Students who initially enter college with the intention of majoring in science, technology, engineering, or mathematics have substantially lower completion rates in these disciplines than do their peers who enter with aspirations for a non-STEM major (Huang et al. 2000). Compounding this problem, under-represented racial minority students in STEM have extremely low bachelor's degree completion rates, especially when compared with their White and Asian American counterparts. A Higher Education Research Institute report indicated that just 24% of White students and 32% of Asian American students who entered college with the intention of majoring in a STEM field completed a bachelor's degree in STEM within four years while 15% of Latino, 13% of Black, and 14% of Native American students did the same (HERI 2010).

Given the low retention and degree completion rates of students who initially choose to major in STEM, policymakers have called for STEM faculty to help retain students by engaging students in innovative strategies that aim to enhance scientific competencies both inside and outside of the classroom (Committee on Science, Engineering, and Public Policy, 2007). The UL LS-LAMP program in its attempt to alleviate this problem encourages students to take advantage of undergraduate research opportunities that apply classroom knowledge to real world problems. The benefits of this form of research participation has shown that students who are involved have an improved ability to think and work like a scientist, clarification of career plans, improved preparedness or desire for graduate study, and higher STEM retention

rates (Espinosa, 2009; Hunter et al., 2006; Laursen et al., 2010; Seymour et al., 2004).

To accomplish the goals related to research exposure:

1. STEM faculty engages students in research projects at UL Lafayette and travel to conferences to present research.

2. LS-LAMP scholars who are involved in research are required to make presentations at professional conferences and LS-LAMP meetings.

3. Summer research opportunities are encouraged and participants are assisted in completing the necessary paperwork to attain positions.

4. LS-LAMP staff assists students in securing the necessary letters of recommendation for research opportunities.

Development of a Professional Culture

Introducing students to essential attitudes and behaviors of professionalism is the primary goal of the activities exposing students to discussions centered on ethics in science. Participants are given access to STEM working papers in magazines, and technical journals.

1. LS-LAMP students are given a list of all professional STEM organizations.
2. Scholars are encouraged to join and provide a listing each semester of all active memberships in STEM organizations.
3. Scholars are asked to provide notification of positions they held within these professional organizations.
4. Attendance and presentations at professional conferences are recommended and funded when the students are presenting.
5. Workshops by STEM faculty regarding the University's specific codes, rules, and policies relating to research ethics.

Development of Computer and Technological Skills

A focus is on LS-LAMP students developing individual, professional web pages. Other activities that forward the goal of insuring that LS-LAMP students develop computer and technological skill development include:

1. All LS-LAMP students participate in the LS-LAMP Facebook Page development and updates. Students are encouraged to ask questions to homework problems or to set up study groups. Building advocacy and exposure of

the program through this social network medium has proven to be extremely beneficial. LS-LAMP staff are able to keep in touch with former students through this venue.

2. All LS-LAMP scholars have established email addresses.
3. Workshops by the co-coordinator of the program include information on search engines, computer visualization, big data
4. Workshops through the Student Support Services Program include information and training on PowerPoint, Excel, Access and SharePoint.

Monitoring

Each LS-LAMP participant is pre-selected, interviewed, and must complete the application for participation in the program. At the time of selection potential scholars are asked to submit:

1. Career goals;
2. Plans after graduation;
3. Brief essay outlining their background, career objectives within 5-10 years, and a brief description of how LS-LAMP might assist them in accomplishing these goals; and
4. Freshmen and sophomores are required to submit an essay outlining a new technology in their respective discipline. Sophomores and juniors must submit a resume along with a cover letter for a prospective job in their field. Seniors must submit an essay, presentation or poster display on the importance of attending graduate school, or an undergraduate research topic.

Scholars check in with the program assistant on a weekly basis to discuss with how classes are proceeding and to address any concerns, tutoring needs or personal concerns. Scholars must meet with the LS-LAMP coordinator the week before the

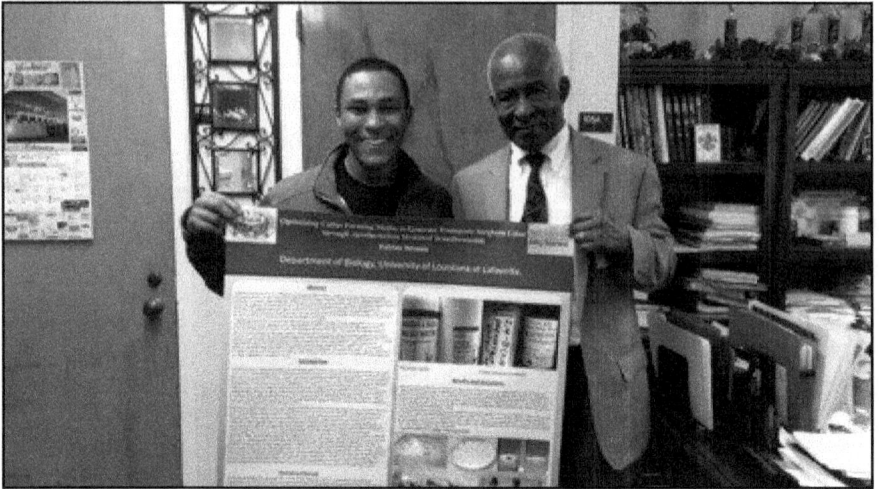

drop date to check the status of all current classes. Grade checks and student progress are assessed at the end of each semester and evaluation of the progress of each LS-LAMP scholar is assessed.

Mentors in each STEM department maintain files on their LS-LAMP scholar documenting information that is kept such as permanent home addresses, emails, telephone numbers, and notes from meetings with mentees. The LS-LAMP office also maintains this information.

Guidance to Graduate School

Beginning freshman year, LS-LAMP staff, advisors and mentors stress the rewards of an exciting time of both personal and intellectual growth, they reinforce the fact that it is also very demanding and requires discipline and focus. Program activities are designed to help scholars develop the personal characteristics coping mechanisms, persistence, and resilience and adequate support systems effective mentors, supportive family, and friends to rely on through the inevitably stressful times. Scholars are required to meet with their mentors to discuss the rigors of graduate school and to get advice from them on how to succeed in this environment. Their mentors are important sources of advice, professional contacts, and the letters of recommendations that they will need.

Program activities that assist in insuring that LS-LAMP scholars are prepared for the rigors of graduate school include:

1. Opportunities to conduct research in the following areas: NSF Research Experiences for Undergraduates (OREUs) CRA-W/CDC Distributed Research Experience for Undergraduates; DRA-W/CDC Collaborative Research Experiences for Undergraduates

2. Workshops for graduate application that delineate: application process; deciding where to go; academic climate; skills; academic credentials; research abilities; GPA; test scores; and financial requirements

3. Other questions to consider when choosing a graduate program; for example:
   - Does the faculty exhibit special strengths and research qualities through their graduate advisees, published works, and funded research?
   - Are the libraries, laboratories, computers and other research facilities adequate for your educational needs?
   - What are the degree requirements?
   - Number of hours of coursework required?
   - What is the completion rate of the general graduate population? Of the female or minority graduate?
   - Does the university have a statement of diversity or an Office of Diversity or Multi-Cultural Affairs?

Conclusion

Increasing the success of racial and ethnic minority students in science, technology, engineering, and mathematics has become a critical issue. Indeed, several trends underscore the importance of fostering success among minority students in STEM education. For example, according to U.S. Census Bureau projections, racial and ethnic minorities are expected to comprise more than half of the national population by 2050. This demographic shift means that minority students will make up an increasingly larger%age of students in the national education system and STEM talent pool. Yet, relatively low rates of success among minority students in STEM education persist. Thus, understanding how to maximize success among racial and ethnic minorities in STEM education is evermore critical. The Ten-Strand Systemic Mentoring Model is a comprehensive system that is interlaced into the core of the program. If implementation of this model is done with fidelity systemic change that makes a difference will occur. The goals and objectives of the UL Lafayette LS-LAMP Program activities implement these key components of the mentoring model, and have produced measurable student outcomes based on evaluation and success.

References

Bunch, G. (2009). "Going up there": Challenges and opportunities for language minority students during a mainstream classroom speech event. Linguistics and Education: An International Research Journal, 20 (2), 81–108.

Committee on Science, Engineering, and Public Policy. (2007). Rising above the gathering storm: Energizing and employing America for a brighter economic future. Retrieved February 25, 2008, from National Academies Press website, http://www.nap.edu/cata- log/11463.html

Espinosa, L. (2009). Pipelines and pathways: Women of color in STEM majors and the experiences that shape their persistence. Unpublished doctoral dissertation.

Higher Education Research Institute. (2010). Degrees of success: Bachelor's degree completion rates among initial STEM majors. Retrieved on March 1, 2010, from http://www.heri.ucla.edu/nih/ HERI_Research-Brief_OL_2010_STEM.pdf

Huang, G., Taddese, N., Walter, E. (2000). Entry and persistence of women and minorities in college science and engineering education (No. NCES 2000601). Washington, D.C.: National Center for Educa- tion Statistics.

Hunter, A. B., Laursen, S. L., Seymour, E. (2006). Becoming a scientist: The role of undergraduate research in students' cognitive, personal, and profession-al development. Science Education, 91(1), 36–74

Kaltenbaugh, L. S., St. John, E. P., and Starkey, J. B. "What Difference Does Tu-ition Make? An Analysis of Ethnic Differences in Persistence." Journal of Student Financial Aid, 1999, 29(2), 21–31.

Ladson-Billings, G. (1995). Toward a theory of culturally relevant pedagogy. American Educational Research Journal, 32 (3), 465– 491.

Laursen, S., Seymour, E., Hunter, A. B., Thiry, H., Melton, G. (2010). Undergrad-uate research in the sciences: Engaging students in real science. San Francisco: Jossey-Bass.

Seymour, E., Hunter, A.B.., Laursen, S., Deantoni, T. (2004). Establishing the benefits of research experiences for undergraduates in the sciences: First findings from a three-year study. Science Education, 88(4), 493–534.

BEST PRACTICES IN SYSTEMIC STEM MENTORING AT UNIVERSITY OF NEW ORLEANS

Ashok Puri, Ph.D.

The U.S. Census Bureau estimates that African Americans, Hispanics and American Indians account for 30% of the U.S. population but are underrepresented in technological fields. The Bureau estimates that by 2050, minorities will comprise half (50%) of the US population. Minorities therefore will be expected to comprise half of the labor force in technological fields or a shortage of scientists and engineers may result (Peng and Hill, 1994). One of the popular way to ensure minority retention is through mentoring. (Jacobi, 1991; Hurte, 2002; Stromei, 2000). Since mentoring immerses the student in the knowledge and experience necessary to practice certain profession, it cannot be acquired from a classroom easily (Engstrom, 2000). Blackwell [5] discusses that only one out of eight African-American students had mentors. Thus there is great need of mentors. Most of the literature confirms that focus of mentoring is on graduate population where professor serves as a mentor to the graduate student[2]. In depth look at the mentoring of graduate student of color is given by Brown et al [6]. Finally, Boyer's research [7] reveals that mentoring of minorities at the universities is rare. We believe that a comprehensive mentoring program is an essential ingredient for student success and mentoring should always be encouraged.

Louisiana at a Glance

There is a stronger need of mentoring in STEM disciplines in Louisiana. In past twenty-three years, only fifteen African Americans and five Hispanics in Louisiana, who received undergraduate degrees in physics went on to complete Ph.D.

Urban Setting

The University of New Orleans is an urban commuter based university. The student population is about 11,000 with 20% being African American. One-third of all science, mathematics, and engineering majors are underrepresented minority, namely African Americans and Hispanic. The population of metropolitan New Orleans is more than 40% African American.

Addressing the underlying student weakness and proposed solutions.The chief underlying weakness that undergraduate minority students in all STEM (science, mathematics, engineering, and technology) disciplines typically face: Under-preparation in mathematics and physics. During 1995-2005 (pre-Katrina) about 300 students participated in summer mentoring program. Summer workshops designed to enhance foundation skills in mathematics and Physics were conducted: identifying student specific needs, and then provide individualized attention in detail. These workshops have multiple objectives: a) provide enrichment in mathematics and physics, b) work closely with students in an informal manner, which is very different from regular classroom instruction, and c) always follow-up. Some of the workshops are summarized below:

- Mathematics: A pre-calculus workshop was created to build and enhance foundations in algebra, trigonometry, and analytical geometry and also to sharpen problem solving skills;
- "Physics: An overview" workshop is conducted to introduce and sharpen fundamental understanding of laws of physics which govern our every day universe. Physics Laboratory workshop (Algebra based run in conjunction with "Physics--overview workshop"). Students go through this workshop two hours per day, four days per week, they learn concepts of error analysis and basic laboratory techniques i.e., how to write the project reports etc.
- Physics/mathematics-Vector Algebra workshop, two hours per day, five days a week was conducted to sharpen the foundation skills of students, vector analysis is fundamental to physics, mathematics, computer science and all engineering disciplines.

Some of the students may opt to work in the recently established Instructional Optics/Laser Laboratory instead of the Vector Analysis workshop and acquire state-of-the-art laboratory skills.

Juniors/Seniors participate in Summer Research Opportunities program. Students present their research findings at National conferences. Students with strong GPAs serve as tutors in mathematics and physics. GRE preparation workshops were offered to students who are considering graduate schools.

Overview

UNO graduated 185 minority STEM graduates during a five-year period just before hurricane Katrina. In contrast, post Katrina data indicates UNO graduated 220 minority STEM graduates during a five-year period just after Katrina. Thus, minority STEM graduations at UNO increased by about 20% compared to pre-Katrina data, whereas minority data for Louisiana, showed an overall decline in STEM graduates by 20% . In light of Hurricane Katrina, this is a significant piece of news for UNO!

LAMP Alumni News

Three minority UNO LS-LAMP alumni completed STEM doctorates in 2011. This is a testimony to the high quality STEM education and training they received while at UNO.

Jolene Robin, who earned a B.S. in electrical engineering and M.S. in applied physics from UNO graduated from Stanford University with a doctorate in geosciences. While an undergraduate student at UNO, she participated in summer research through the SULI program at Stanford University.

Abby Wood, who earned a B.S. in physics with a biology minor from UNO, graduated with doctorate in medical physics from the University of Chicago (May 2011). She is a medical physicist at MD Anderson Cancer Center, Houston TX. While as undergraduate student at UNO, she participated in summer Research at Stanford University through the SULI/DOE program.

Sydeaka Watson, who earned a B.S. in mathematics, graduated from Los Alamos National Laboratory/Baylor University (May 2011) Ph.D. in bio-statistics. Currently, Watson is an assistant pro-

fessor of health sciences at the University of Chicago. While at UNO, Sydeaka participated in summer research at Michigan State University, where she later completed a M.S. degree in mathematics.

All of these students worked as peer tutors in mathematics and physics while at UNO. These graduates are a source of inspiration and encouragement to our current and future LS-LAMP scholars.

Highlights

Fifty-one minority students graduated in STEM from UNO in 2010-2011 year. This number is an all-time high over the past ten years.

LS-LAMP scholar, Daphne Meza, mechanical engineering major, accepted through SULI/DOE summer research program at Brookhaven National Laboratory, summer 2011.

LS-LAMP Scholar, Daniel Duarte, physics major, was selected to participate in the Ronald McNair Scholar program at LSU,

2010, where he worked on a project related to deep water Horizon project, examining X-ray spectroscopy of crude oil samples, testing for toxic substance like Vanadium and Nickel. (Graduate student, Jamal Alexander, was selected as a GEM Scholar.) Two UNO LS-LAMP scholars presented at an undergraduate research conference organized by AAAS, Washington DC, Feb. 2011. One of the presenters earned a full travel scholarship. Four LS-LAMP scholars presented their findings at the undergraduate research conference held at Arizona State University, Feb. 2011. Twenty-two LS-LAMP scholars receive book awards. (LS-LAMP book awards—total $250 per semester—require semester GPA of 3.0 or better.) This clearly indicates improvement in quality of minority STEM students at UNO. An engineering/physics student from Xavier, LeAndre Foster joined UNO under 3-2 engineering program.

In order to streamline and optimize student graduations, LS-LAMP supports STEM minority students for summer school Tuition. In summer 2011, fifteen students received summer tuition awards.

Pre-Hurricane Katrina Mentoring Activities
Basics Summer Workshop
Basics--a workshop designed to enhance fundamental skills in mathematics and physics was conducted: (1) a "Physics: An Overview" workshop was conducted to introduce and sharpen fundamental understanding of the laws of physics, which govern our everyday world. Emphasis was given to foundations in algebra, trigonometry, and analytic geometry and also to sharpen problem-solving skills; and (2) physics laboratory workshop (algebra-based) was conducted in conjugation with above course. Students developed deeper appreciation of concepts in error analysis.

Goals and Objectives

To provide students with instructional support--as a basic course in "Overview of Physics" including a laboratory workshop and to assist them in developing comprehensive mathematical/ laboratory skills which are essential for any science and engineering fields.

Advanced Summer Workshop

Advanced--a preparatory undergraduate research and upper level coursework in physics and mathematical physics with emphasis on vector algebra is strongly emphasized. This LS-LAMP junior and senior-level component consists of a workshop. The workshop is designed to provide fundamental skills in vector calculus, techniques needed for all STEM majors. Topics covered typically are: coordinates and vector algebra, derivatives and differential, the gradient, integration along a path, circulation and curl, flux and derivatives, Integral theorems and related physical applications.

Activity Goals and Participation

To provide students with instructional support as a basic workshop in vector analysis and to assist them in developing comprehensive mathematical skills which are essential for any science and engineering fields. Thus preparing students for more regroups academic schedule in fall.

Summer Projects

Students work on summer projects in area of their discipline. These projects were carried out as a part of the summer program. Both basic and advanced students participated in summer projects. Students study a specific topic and develop into a

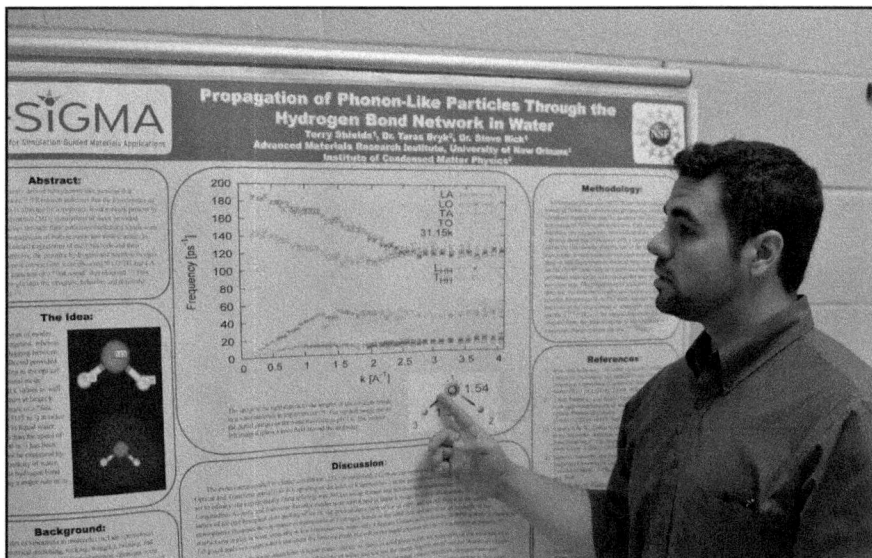

project. They display their findings in form of project board and present their work to their peers and project coordinators. Both Basics and Advanced participants completed summer projects.

Activity Goals and Participation

The prime objective of working on a project is to develop deeper understanding on a specific topic of investigation. Student does independent literature search, conducts their research draws conclusions from his or her findings. Writing a scientific project report should assist student develop technical writing skills.

Conference Participation

Students are expected to present their findings at research conferences. Students will present their research at DOE EP-SCoR, NAFEO, APS, and ACS conferences. Conferences always

have a graduate school attendance session that provides students with valuable information on graduate school programs at a large number of universities.

Activity Goals and Participation
Students will learn about current research in diverse fields in various STEM disciplines. Presentation of their findings will assist students develop advanced communication skills. Networking is one of the most important aspects of conference participation. Students will interact with DOE, and other national laboratory representatives for future internship prospects. Students will be encouraged to seek out graduate school admission opportunities.

Summer Internships

This activity is designed primarily to concentrate on juniors and seniors. Students will apply to CIC (Committee on Institutional Cooperation), DOE Research Laboratories, and NSF for summer research experiences. Students will interview and establish contact with CIC caravan when they visit New Orleans in February for Summer Research Opportunities Program (SROP) and recruit for graduate school admissions.

Activity Goals and Participation
The primary objective is to expose students in their junior year to the state-of-the-art research environment. Such a summer research experience will assist students build strong research background and encourage students to eventually consider going to graduate schools. Furthermore contacts built through SROP program should be extremely helpful to students when they apply for graduate schools, go for site visits, and complete other activities.

Tutoring

This activity is designed primarily to concentrate on freshmen and sophomores with lower GPAs. Students who are perceived to be weak (2.7 or lower GPA in major courses) or recommended by their faculty advisers are required to take advantage of the tutoring services. Our stronger students primarily juniors and seniors devote time (approximately) four hours a week at the Learning Resource Center and in individual departments to provide tutoring. Currently, tutoring is provided in physics and mathematics.

Activity Goals and Objectives

To provide freshmen and sophomore students develop study skills. Spending time at the Learning Resource center assists student develop study discipline. Physics and Mathematics are the building blocks of all STEM majors. Tutoring in these areas will provide students help in developing their basic background. Building student background in the area of pre-Calculus is significant. Freshmen and sophomores are paired with juniors and seniors. This results in close interaction between beginners and advanced students and fosters a collaborative learning environment. Tutoring others helps tutors clarify and reinforce their own knowledge in major STEM subjects. They will develop better communication skills through tutoring.

Book Awards

LS-LAMP UNO has instituted a performance based reward system. Book awards are given to minority STEM students for good semester GPA. Students must take at least one major course in a given semester and must at least score B level performance in the major course, and must at least have a semester

B average to be eligible for book award. Minority students in STEM disciplines are eligible for book award of $100 and $200, respectively both during Fall and Spring semesters. These awards are available through UNO Bookstore as books of equivalent amount, and not in form of cash.

Activity Goals and Objectives

The objectives of this activity are to offer book awards to encourage current students who show improvement in their GPA. Book awards are based on semester GPA only. Thus good performance in a semester is rewarded immediately. Provide incentive to new students to join enrichment program.

Summer Research Opportunities Program

STEM minority students in their junior year are expected to seek Summer Research Opportunities at top Research Universities and National laboratories. LS-LAMP scholars are encouraged to apply to Committee on Institutional Cooperation/Summer Research Opportunities Program. Applications are completed in early spring for coming summer. We have been successful in motivating significant number of STEM minority scholars to apply for summer research program. During pre-Katrina years approximately, thirty UNO students apply to the program and approximately ten students are accepted. CIC does an excellent job in matching student interests with mentors at fifteen participating Midwestern Universities. Student's application and recommendations are submitted online and are available for review by participating CIC partner institutions.

Louisiana Board of Regents' Support Fund Graduate Fellows Scholarship Program

During the first ten years of the LS-LAMP program, Board of Regents of the State of Louisiana funded Department of Physics of University of New Orleans established superior graduate fellowships to support the master of science degree in physics at the University of New Orleans. In recent years, we have been successful in receiving funding for four fellowships for recruiting Superior Masters Students. All four Fellows were minority and women minority.

Enhanced Instructional Optics/Laser Laboratory at University of New Orleans

We established Instructional Optics laboratory at the University of New Orleans via by two separate curriculum Enhancement grants from Louisiana Board of Regents. Primary objective has been to establish state-of-the art laboratory. Minority STEM students from various science and engineering disciplines go through hands-on state–of-the-art experiences. In 2003, a fiber optics component was added to the instructional laboratory.

Exposing students to higher caliber fiber optics experiments that have clear industry marketability will lead to well trained students. Intensive preparation of undergraduate students will improve the probability of going to graduate schools. National Science Foundation has high priority for improvement of minority access to science and mathematics education. This enhanced optics laboratory clearly enhances that goal.

Institutional Commitment to STEM

In order to address retention at the University level, UNO is currently implementing a University Success course with exclu-

sive sections designed for science majors encouraging research. College of Sciences (CoS) at UNO offers robust Research opportunities program during the school year. Students from all science disciplines are encouraged to participate in this program. This is a great opportunity available to UNO science students enhancing their STEM experience at UNO.

Community College Outreach and Recruitment

One of the LS-LAMP requirements is to develop close community college interaction and encourage minority STEM students to transfer to four-year schools. We conducted week long work shop with ten STEM minority students from Nunez and Delgado community colleges wishing to transfer to UNO/other four-year colleges. This resulted in three of them Transferring to UNO (chemistry, biology, and computer science).

Future Direction

It must be underscored that comprehensive mentoring is of absolute necessity for continued success of our students. Timely advisement leads to right sequence of courses a student must take in order to graduate in reasonable time. Instance after instances such advising has saved time and made student's path easier. Equally significant are enrichment workshops in physics and mathematics, conference participation and participation in summer research programs at top research universities and national laboratories. We continue many of the pre-Katrina mentoring activities in post-Katrina environment. Most recently, Community college component has been added to our mentoring effort. The idea is to encourage more community college students to transfer to the four-year college. Currently, STEM workshops are being planned to enhance community college interaction.

Acknowledgement

Thank you to LS-LAMP program director and distinguished professor at Southern University and A&M College, Diola Bagayoko, Ph.D., for his close guidance, and allowing the participating campuses to use the ten strands of highly successful mentoring practices outlined on Timbuktu Academy and LS-LAMP websites.

References

[1] Characteristics and educational experiences of high-achieving minority students in science and mathematics, P. Peng and S. Hill, Journal of Women and Minorities in Science and Engineering, 1 (2), 137-152 (1994).

[2] Mentoring and Undergraduate Academic success: A literature review, M. Jacobi, Review of Educational Research, 61(4), 505-32 (1991).

[3] Mentoring: the forgotten retention tool, V. J. Hurte, Black issues in Higher Education 19 (18) 49 (2002).

[4] Increasing retention and success through mentoring, L. K. Stromei , New Direction for Community Colleges, no 112,San Francisco. Jossey-Bass. (2000)

[5] Mentoring: An action strategy for increasing minority faculty, J. Blackwell, Academe 75, 8-14 (1989).

[6] Mentoring Graduate Students of Color: Myths, Models, and Modes, M. Christopher Brown II and Guy L. Davis and Shederick A. McClendon, Peabody Journal of Education, 74(2), 105-118 (1999).

[7] College: The Undergraduate Experience in America, E. Boyer, New York (1987).

[8] Derived data from the WebCASPAR database located at http://webcaspar.nsf.gov/includes/checkJavascriptAbility2.jsp;jsessionid=FFA3F2F865566B6ABF-F18381819488C9?submitted=1

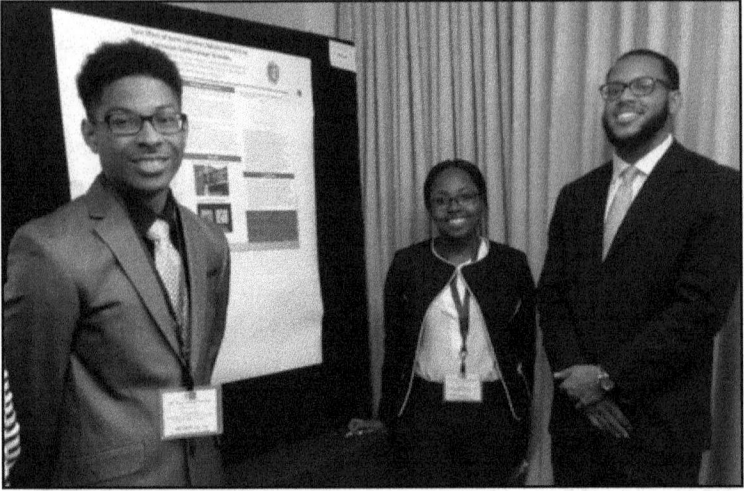

Best Practices in Systemic STEM Mentoring At Xavier University

Murty Akundi and Syed Muniruzzaman, Ph.D.

Xavier University of Louisiana is a historically Black and Catholic institution nationally recognized for its science, technology, engineering and mathematics curriculum, while remaining close to its liberal arts roots. Xavier's mission is to create a more just and humane society by preparing its students to assume roles of leadership and service in a global society. This preparation takes place in a diverse learning and teaching environment that incorporates all relevant educational means, including research and community service.

As of Fall 2011, the University has 240 full-time faculty members who offer courses in 44 majors on the undergraduate, graduate, and first-professional degree levels. With a record breaking

4,121 students prior to Katrina, current enrollment is 3,399, 74% are African American. 2,587 students are enrolled in the College of Arts and sciences, with 623 students enrolled in the College of Pharmacy, which offers the Doctor of Pharmacy Degree. Master's programs in the graduate school enroll 183 students. Approximately 57% of Xavier students are from Louisiana, primarily from the New Orleans area. The balance comes from 37 other states coast-to-coast, the District of Columbia, the Virgin Islands, and several countries.

According to the U.S. Department of Education, Xavier, during the past decade, has ranked first nationally in the number of African-American students earning undergraduate degrees in biology, chemistry, physics, and the physical sciences overall. 70% of undergraduate students major in the sciences. Many well-prepared, highly motivated students are attracted by Xavier's reputation in this regard. Conversely, academically disadvantaged students also are drawn to Xavier because of its track record in "leveling the playing field," especially in the first year of college. The New York Times Selective Guide to Colleges observes, "Xavier is a school where achievement has been the rule, and beating the odds against success a routine occurrence."

Recent data shows that Xavier also is national leader in the number of its STEM majors who go on to receive doctorates. According to National science Foundation statistics, Xavier currently ranks ninth in the nation in producing African American students who go on to earn science and engineering (S&E) Ph.D.s. Between 2004 and 2008, forty-nine of Xavier's graduates earned their doctorates in S&E fields .

Xavier also has a national reputation in producing health professionals. Since 1993, Xavier has been first in the nation in placing African-American students into medical schools. The 77%

acceptance rate of Xavier graduates is almost twice the national average, and 92% of those who enter medical school from Xavier complete their degrees. The College of Pharmacy has also consistently been among the nation's leaders in awarding doctor of pharmacy degrees to African Americans.

Goals and Objectives

National studies point to the decreasing numbers of U.S. students enrolling in science and engineering at both the undergraduate and graduate levels. One of the greatest potential sources for increasing the number of scientists and engineers is the U.S. African-American population. African Americans obtain far fewer science degrees than should be the case, given their percentage of the U.S. population. In mathematics, engineering, and the life and physical sciences, less than 10% of the bachelor's degrees, less than 7% of the master's degrees, and less than 3% of the doctoral degrees are conferred to African Americans. According to NSF statistics, about 53% of African Americans versus 68% of Caucasians attend college, while 19% of African Americans versus 37% of Caucasians graduate. Currently, African Americans represent 12% of the US population, but only 3% of the STEM workforce. These small%ages can be attributed to a number of factors including urban school systems that do not adequately prepare African Americans in mathematics and science disciplines and, at the university level, a lack of student-focused curricula, faculty mentoring and effective advising.

The long term goals of the Louis-Stokes Louisiana Alliance for Minority Participation program are: 1) to increase the number and quality of minority students receiving bachelor's degrees in STEM disciplines and 2) to increase proportionately the number of LS-LAMP alumni in graduate program. Xavier's national reputation in graduating African-American undergraduates in STEM fields and sending them on to graduate school uniquely positions us to participate fully in the LS-LAMP program. To achieve this level of success, Xavier utilizes the LS-LAMP Systemic Mentoring Model which includes comprehensive academic advising, tutoring, research participation, guidance to graduate school, professional development and financial support for students. The following sections describe how Xavier University of Louisiana engages in each of the ten strands of the Systemic Mentoring Model.

Financial Support

The LS-LAMP program provides student stipends in the amount of $3,000 for a total of eight Xavier undergraduates annually to participate in the program. In addition, Xavier's Office of Financial Aid, Office of Resource Development, and Academic Affairs staff, as well as STEM department chairs, distribute information on scholarships, fellowships, and other external funding opportunities to all STEM students at the University.

As a form of cost-sharing, the University provides scholarships to approximately four or five LS-LAMP scholars annually. During the summers, LS-LAMP students are afforded the opportunity to participate in internships though Xavier's formal partnerships with several universities and national labs across the country, including the University of Wisconsin - Madison Synchrotron Radiation Center, Tulane University, University of Minnesota, Indiana University, and North Carolina State University. Through these mechanisms, students are provided with the financial support necessary to focus on their studies, research, and related enrichment activities on a full-time basis, without dividing their time or relying on outside employment for financial support.

Communication Skill Enhancement

Strong oral and written communication skills are important for future STEM leaders. To facilitate the development of these skills, LS-LAMP scholars have access to the University's Writing Center, which provides assistance with general or specific areas of the writing process, including developing personal statements for medical school, graduate school, internships, and scholarships, and classroom tutorials on critical writing strategies. These writing skills are utilized both in STEM classes and through a required written progress report that each student must develop at the end of the academic year detailing the findings of their research projects. Faculty mentors work with students on editing these reports and provide important training on technical writing. To develop oral communication skills, all LS-LAMP scholars are required to present their research findings at Xavier's Festival of Scholars program arranged by the Center for Undergraduate Research. The students are also encouraged to present at national conferences and the annual LS-LAMP conference. Through these activities, students are exposed to a variety of technical communication methods and in turn, begin to enhance their scientific reading, writing and presentation skills.

Comprehensive Scientific Advisement

Each STEM student at Xavier is assigned a faculty mentor to monitor student's progress throughout the year. Students are expected to meet with their advisor every two weeks with their advisor card in which the student will enter his/her grade in the courses taken in that semester. Faculty mentors will advise the students who earned a D or less in particular subject to attend the tutoring center and report the progress in the next meeting. To

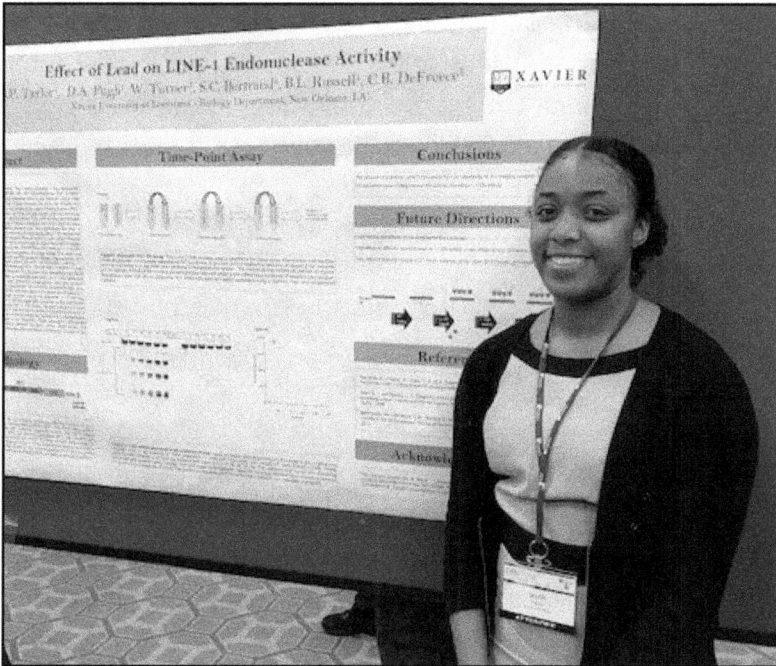

continue in the LS-LAMP program at Xavier, students must maintain a minimum cumulative GPA of 2.75. The University also provides support and training to new faculty on how to appropriately mentor and advise students through the Center for the Advancement of Teaching. These comprehensive, scientific advisement activities are central to the success of the undergraduate student.

Tutoring

Each STEM department at Xavier has established tutoring centers with exemplary STEM students standing as tutors trained by faculty members. Students meet with tutors approximately once a week. Xavier's upper level LS-LAMP scholars are paired with NSF HBCU-UP freshman students to assist them in acclimating to the University culture. In addition, students may participate in problem solving, career, study skill, and time management workshops through the Counseling Center. Through peer tutoring, our LS-LAMP scholars reinforce their own knowledge and promote their communication skills by training other students.

Generic Research Activities

Through research laboratories and enhanced STEM curricula, Xavier's undergraduates are students are introduced to research tools and methods, including the scientific method and additional critical thinking skills. Faculty increase student knowledge and skills by using some of the best practices and innovative teaching approaches. These include implementing active learning, developing more interesting and engaging activities for honing students' computational and critical thinking skills, revising labs to add more open-ended exercises and more data interpretation assignments to improve students' reasoning and analytical abilities, and revamping applicable lab courses to include discovery/research-oriented projects using courses such as the HHMI funded 'Phage genomics' course as a model. Xavier is committed to implementing a more student-centered style of teaching, emphasizing application of knowledge as opposed to rote memorization.

Specific Research Project Execution

To help facilitate undergraduate research, Xavier created CUR with the responsibility of engaging more undergraduate students in research and in mentoring relationships with Xavier faculty. NSF studies have shown that involving freshman and sophomore students in research increases the likelihood of them becoming

STEM majors, and involving them in research in their junior and senior years makes them more likely to go onto graduate school in STEM fields.

With the assistance of CUR, faculty mentors are selected for each of the LS-LAMP scholars based on their research interests. Students are expected to conduct research with faculty for at least 10 hours per week. Students are required to present their research findings at Xavier's annual Festival of Scholars, and prepare a written report analyzing their findings. Students are also required to participate in off-campus summer research at another university or government/private research facility. To facilitate these experiences, Xavier hosts an REU program for students interested in conducting research in organic chemistry, analytical chemistry, materials science, and molecular biology.

Development of a Professional Culture

Students have the opportunity to strengthen their professional skills through a variety of activities. Several student-run STEM clubs and professional organizations are active within the various STEM disciplines. LS-LAMP scholars are encouraged to join these organizations and participate in a meaningful way. They are also encouraged to regularly read technical journals and travel with their faculty mentors to scientific meetings and professional conferences. Students have the opportunity to publish the results of their research courses and summer and academic year research in Xavier's peer-reviewed journal, XULAneXUS. These professional development activities will be incredibly valuable in helping the students to transition from undergraduate learning to graduate school and STEM careers.

Computer and Technological Skills

Mastery of computational skills is necessary for all STEM students. Xavier's Office of technology Administration and Information technology Center provides workshops to students on computer applications such as PowerPoint, Excel, or any other relevant software. In addition, Xavier's curriculum has been developed to increase students' computer literacy beginning at the freshman level through in-class computer activities. The computer science department is working more closely with other STEM departments to effectively use creative technologies to enrich STEM learning. Xavier has also been building up the number of students trained at high-performance computing through a gran from the National Science Foundation which includes HPC research and educational activities for faculty and undergraduates, as well as funding to connect Xavier to the Louisiana Optical Network Initiative, a high-speed fiber optics network that connects all of the research universities in the State.

Monitoring

Xavier monitors its students through the use of advisor cards, which include a mentoring portfolio on each student. These cards serve to evaluate student progress, make sure students remain on track to graduate, monitor class attendance and attendance in computer labs. Students are required to meet with their mentors every two weeks to review their progress. In order to improve retention and graduation rates, Xavier's Office of Student Academic Success provides monitoring and advising to students who are academically at risk. Students receive academic support through the coordination, enhancement, and support of peer tutoring and academic labs. Xavier's 'Early Alert' system is utilized to offer un-

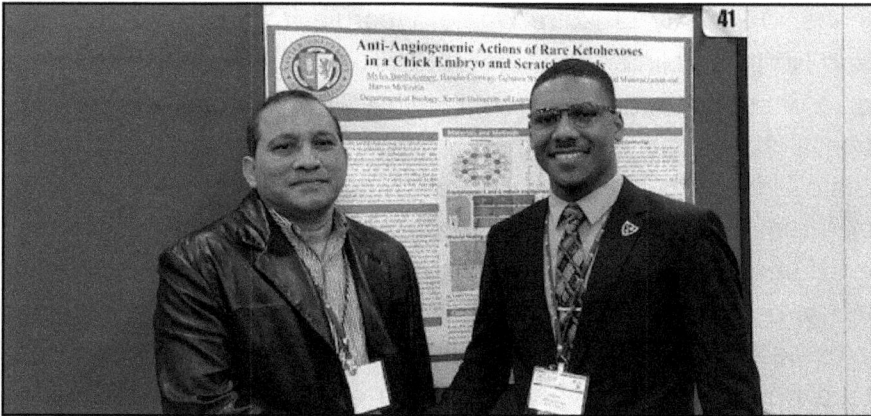

derperforming students the resources to help boost their confidence, academic performance and retention.

This system requires instructors to offer feedback on students' performance, behavior, attendance and any other possible concerns to a central database where it is analyzed and results are communicated to both the teachers and the students. Identified students are contacted and advised to attend the tutoring centers and are informed about other applicable support systems or educational resources available on campus.

Guidance to Graduate School

The Office of Graduate Placement was established at Xavier University to promote interest and encourage students to pursue graduate studies. This office arranges graduate school visits for thirty to forty students annually. The Office of Graduate Placement is instrumental in arranging graduate record examination preparation workshops. The Writing Center and Office of Graduate Placement staff and faculty mentors assist students with graduate school applications. Xavier has established a dual degree engineering program with Tulane University, University of New Orleans, University of Notre Dame, Georgia Institute of technology and North Carolina A&T State University. Each of these institutions also offers graduate programs in the STEM disciplines. In addition, Xavier has established collaborations with Pennsylvania State University, New York University, and Indiana State University. These institutions have reasonable minority enrollment in their graduate programs and established support programs to nurture the progress of Xavier students. The collaborating institutions provide opportunities for minority students at Xavier University to take courses and conduct research at these institutions during their junior and senior years. Through this program, students are given an opportunity to learn more about the institution and have a greater chance of success in the graduate program.

Conclusion

Minorities currently represent an expanding portion of the U.S. population. Unless STEM education becomes more inclusive, our increasingly technological society will soon be denied the talents of a large segment of our population. Increasing the number of African Americans graduating in STEM disciplines and moving on to graduate school is one of the primary goals on which Xavier University has been focusing for two decades. Through the LS-LAMP program and the Ten-Strand Systemic Mentoring Model, Xavier is creating a pipeline of underrepresented undergraduates who are well trained and qualified for graduate school and life-long careers in STEM fields. These initiatives build on Xavier's national excellence in graduating African-American scientists and provide students with the skills necessary to guarantee their success in graduate school at any research-oriented university.

ABOUT THE AUTHORS

OLUSEGUN ADEYEMI, PH.D.

Olusegun Adeyemi, Ph.D., is the head of Grambling State University's Department of Engineering Technology, a position he has held since arriving at GSU in July 2008. Since arriving at GSU, Adeyemi has lead his department to a successful reaffirmation of two ABET-accredited programs. He serves on two President's Advisory Committees: Title III and Sponsored Programs Advisory Committee and the A. C. Lewis Library Advisory Committee. These are two of the 12 university wide committees charged to develop and recommend initiatives to assist with accomplishing university priorities. Adeyemi served one year as co-coordinator of GSU LS-LAMP program before taking over as campus coordinator in August 2012. Adeyemi's previous academic experience includes eight and half years at Tuskegee University and thirteen and a half years coordinating the dual degree engineering program at Morehouse College in Atlanta, GA. He received multiple awards for teaching excellence and mentoring both at Tuskegee University and Morehouse College. His industrial experience includes work at Portland Cement Company and 3M Company. Adeyemi holds a bachelor's degree from the University of Lagos, Lagos, Nigeria, a master's degree from Stanford University in Palo Alto, CA and a doctorate from the University of Texas in Austin; all in mechanical engineering. His research interests include investigation of the relationship between processing conditions, morphology and mechanical properties of engineering materials, with particular applications to polymer blends and alloys, and analysis and design of intelligent material system.

DIOLA BAGAYOKO, PH.D.

Diola Bagayoko, Ph.D., is Southern University System Distinguished Professor of Physics, Director, the Timbuktu Academy and the Louis Stokes Louisiana Alliance for Minority Participation (LS-LAMP), Dean, the Dolores Margaret Richard Spikes Honors College, Southern University and A&M College in Baton Rouge (SUBR). Dr. Bagayoko earned the BS degree in Physics and Chemistry from the Ecole Normale Supérieure (ENSup) of Bamako, Mali, the MS in Physics from Lehigh University, Bethlehem, Pennsylvania, and the Ph.D. in condensed matter theory from Louisiana State University (LSU). The introduction, with the late Dr. Ella L. Kelley, of the law of human performance and its applications to teaching and learning and to systemic mentoring shaped his career. The systemic mentoring programs he directs, i.e., the Timbuktu Academy and the Louis Stokes Louisiana Alliance for Minority Participation have produced 94, 54, and 80 physics, chemistry, and engineering Bachelor's degree holders, respectively, from 1995 to 2016. Respectively 22, 20, and 20 of these graduates have earned the Ph.D. degree in their fields. Bagayoko and a few colleagues have harnessed $50 million of sponsored funding for scholarships and assistantships, the building of the instructional infrastructure and the integration of technology in teaching and learning, and the support of research. The contents of his 125 and 60 publications in theoretical physics and in teaching, mentoring, and learning (TML), respectively, have been disseminated locally, nationally, and internationally through 579 presentations. His correction of 50 years of misunderstanding of density functional theory (DFT) and his completion of DFT in practice paved the way for the success of the Materials Genome Initiative [AIP Advances, 4, 127104 (2014)]. Dr. Bagayoko received the 1996 US Presidential Award for Excellence in Science, Mathematics, and Engineering Mentoring (US-PAESMEM). The Timbuktu Academy received the 2002 US-PAESMEM. Other national awards of Dr. Bagayoko include the 2009 Life Time Mentor Award from the American Association for the Advancement of Science (AAAS), and the 2007 Benjamin Banneker Legacy and the 2017 BEYA STEM Innovation Awards.

GRETCHEN SCHNEIDER BURTON, Ph.D.

A Louisiana native, Burton served as the LSU LS-LAMP program coordinator and counselor from 2008 to 2013. Dr. Schneider Burton received her Master's in Education in Counselor Education in May 2004 from Southeastern Louisiana University, Education Specialist (Ed.S.) in May 2017 and Ph.D. in Educational Leadership and Research in December 2017 from Louisiana State University. She currently holds a National Certified Counselor Certification with the National Board of Certified Counselors, Louisiana Certificate in School Guidance with the Louisiana Department of Education, and state licensure with the Louisiana Practicing Counselor Board. Her role as LS-LAMP coordinator and counselor is to assist with the scholars educational training program, as well as to track their academic progress. All participants receive academic, career and personal advising. Burton also serves as the program manager and counselor for the Initiative for Maximizing Student Development Program at Louisiana State University since funding began in 2004. The IMSD Program, funded by the National Institutes of Health, provides qualified undergraduates training in biomedical research while enhancing diversity in the biomedical sciences.

MICHAEL CUNNINGHAM, PH.D.

Michael Cunningham, Ph.D, is the campus coordinator for the Louisiana Alliance for Minority Participation at Tulane University. Professor and an association provost for engaged learning and teaching, he also leads the university's Center for Engaged Learning and Teaching. CELT's mission is to enhance student learning and to pursue the development of engagement-based and experiential curriculums across all University Schools and Centers as well as Newcomb-Tulane College. Mike's academic affiliations are with the Department of Psychology and the program in African and African Diaspora Studies at Tulane.

MELISSA CRAWFORD

Melissa Crawford earned her bachelor's degree in chemistry, magna cum laude from LSU, where she served for the past eleven years as a program manager for Howard Hughes Medical Institute Professors (HHMI) Program, the NSF-funded Louisiana Science, Technology, Engineering, and Mathematics (LA-STEM) Research Scholars and Louis Stokes Louisiana Alliance for Minority Participation (LS-LAMP) Programs. Crawford has mentored more than 350 students, employing a holistic development learning approach to create high-quality STEM ambassadors, who go on to complete graduate programs. Crawford has extensive administrative experience at LSU, with strengths in recruitment, motivation, and retention of undergraduates. She is actively involved in areas of increasing student access and success in undergraduate STEM degree programs and broadening the participation of underrepresented groups in STEM. Crawford is the co-developer of a comprehensive Success Course aimed at preparing STEM undergraduates for doctoral programs, STEM careers, leadership, and public service. Crawford has also served the coordinator and instructor for an eight-week Summer Bridge Program and a ten-week NSF-funded REU program. Additionally, she has also been the co-coordinator of the annual LSU Undergraduate Research Conference for the past ten years.

ABDALLA DARWISH, PH.D.

In 2017, Professor Darwish was named the Male faculty of the year from the HBCU' universities by the HBCU digest. Dr. Darwish is a distinguished professor of physics, in 2014 was named Dillard University's Presidential Professor. He is also holds Ruth Simmons University Distinguished University Professor and International Society of Optics and Photonic "SPIE" Fellow. During his tenure at Al A&M University he supervised 7 graduate students (5 MS and 2PhD). He has been a Dillard University faculty member since 1998 and has served Dillard university in numerous administrative roles, including chair of the physics and pre Engineering department, chair of the School of STEM, interim dean of the College of Arts and Sciences, and Associate

Provost and Associate senior Vice President for Academic Affairs. Prof Darwish is an expert in thin film fabrication using the Pulse Laser Deposition technique, Nonlinear optical materials (NLO), Electron paramagnetic Resonance (EPR), Infrared double Optical Spectroscopy, ion implantation, Fabrication of optical, chemical and Bio sensor devices using double and triple PLD concurrent MAPLE thin film fabrication technique which he invented and has seven patents applications pending. Darwish has authored over 100 publications in the areas of nonlinear optical materials, magnetic resonance, waveguides, thin film fabrication and sensors and two chapters books. See (www.researchgate.net) . Under his leadership, the physics department became a signature program for Dillard University, and holds a National standing in graduating more than 55% of African American in physics since 2000 by AIP and second in graduating black females in physics. Darwish has been able to secure over $16.7 million in grant funds to establish many programs and research enterprises in the physics department which was supported by US AFRL, US AFOSR, US Army RO, ARL, NSF and NASA.In addition, Dr. Abdalla Darwish holds a public office where he has been serving as member of city of Kenner civil service board since its inception in 2006 until present. Dr. Darwish was awarded the Monte Lemann Award from the civil service league of the State of LA in Oct 2014. Dr. Darwish has many National and International invitations for seminars, keynote speakers, conference chairs and others. Just in the last five years he delivered over international 25 talks, in US, Spain, canary Island, Japan, China, Italy and France.

BOBBIE DECUIR, PH.D.

Bobbie B. DeCuir, Ph.D., is the interim dean of the College of General Studies and the associate director of Campus Trio Programs that include student support services for students enrolled in science, technology, engineering, and mathematics. In this capacity DeCuir works to ensure that STEM students are given the necessary resources and assistance to successfully complete a degree in these demanding and rigorous curriculum. DeCuir has served as the LS-LAMP co-coordinator at University of Louisiana Lafayette for the past ten years, along with Vijay Raghavan, Ph.D.

LASHOUNDA TORRENCE FRANKLIN

Lashounda Torrence Franklin is the program manager for the Timbuktu Academy and the Senior Research Associate for the SUBR component of LS-LAMP. Valedictorian of St. Helena Central High, she earned a BS degree in Physics from SUBR where she was an undergraduate scholar of the Timbuktu Academy. In 2001, she earned the MS in Physics from SUBR, under the supervision of Diola Bagayoko, PhD. She was a funded Superior Graduate Fellow. She joined the staff of the Academy in 2001. According to the Academy's Directors, her administrative, academic, and other support roles are pivotal ones for the systemic mentoring and scientific research activities of the Academy and LS-LAMP. As a scholar of the Timbuktu Academy, Franklin was immersed in the Academy's systemic mentoring activities, which included full financial support.

During her graduate studies, she conducted research on ab-initio self-consistent calculations of electronic properties of materials. Bagayoko, project director of the Timbuktu Academy, served as her thesis research advisor and thesis committee chairman. After maintaining a 4.0 GPA and successfully defending her research thesis, "The BZW Method and Electronic Properties of Zinc Selenide (ZnSe)." She has conducted ground-breaking research on semi-conductor materials including wurzite Zinc Oxide (w-ZnO), wurzite Indium Nitride (w-InN) and zinc-blende Indium Nitride (zb-InN). With the guidance of Bagayoko and the assistance of Ekuma Chinedu Ekuma PhD., Franklin and her colleagues formulated the internationally recognized "BZW-EF Method." She has extensive training in performing computations and in mentoring undergraduate and graduate students at SUBR. She has authored six (research publications and co-authored more than twenty-five research publications in peer-reviewed journals, including the *Journal of Physics and Chemistry Solids,* the *Journal of Applied Physics*, the *Canadian Journal of Physics,* and the *African Journal of Physics*.

DANNY HUBBARD, PH.D.

Danny Hubbard, Ph.D., is associate dean of the College of Arts and Sciences at Grambling State University. In addition to serving in the capacity of LS-LAMP campus coordinator he is co-PI of the Center for Mathematical Achievement in Science and Technology. The center was established in 2006 and is supported by the National Science Foundation. Hubbard earned a Ph. D. in chemistry from Clark Atlanta University in 1994 with emphasis on coordination/ inorganic polymers;

and was the first African American to earn a Ph.D. from the High Performance Polymer and Composites Center. Recent studies show that polyimides are viable components in high performance polymer and polymer composite applications. Students are involved in synthesis, thermal mechanical studies, and characterization of monomers and polymers receive training in the use of instrumental techniques, e.g., Differential Scanning Calorimetry Thermal Gravimetric Analysis, and (Dynamic) Thermo-mechanical Analysis in the characterization of these materials.

ELLA LEE KELLEY PH.D.

Ella Lee Kelley Ph.D. a trailblazer in science, technology, engineering, and mathematics (STEM) education, was a nationally recognized educator and advocate for STEM education, research, and mentoring. Kelley joined the faculty of the Department of Chemistry at Southern University and A&M College in Baton Rouge (SUBR), Louisiana in 1983. Throughout her more than three decades at SUBR, she served as co-director of the Timbuktu Academy (1990-2015) with her husband, Diola Bagayoko, Ph.D.. She rose through the academic ranks to hold a number of administrative positions, including Chair of the Chemistry Department, Associate Vice Chancellor of Academic Affairs, and Dean of the Dolores Margaret Richard Spikes Honors College. Valedictorian of her high school class, Kelley earned the BS degree in chemistry from the University of Louisiana at Monroe, the master of science in chemistry from SUBR, and the Ph.D. in biochemistry from Louisiana State University in Baton Rouge in 1983. During her tenure as professor of chemistry, she authored or co-authored more than thirty articles in refereed technical publications in biochemistry, teaching, mentoring, and learning. Kelley directed the 2002 U.S. Presidential Award for Excellence in Science Mathematics and Engineering Mentoring for the Timbuktu Academy. She directed and co-directed projects totaling more than $10 million dollars. She was also the co-principal investigator of the Louis Stokes Louisiana Alliance for Minority Participation (LS-LAMP) and Campus Coordinator of the Southern University LS-LAMP Program.

JOSEPHINE POUNCY LOSTON

Josephine P. Loston was born in Shreveport, Louisiana, in Caddo Parish. She grew up in Dallas, Texas, attended school within the Greater Dallas/Forth Worth School System, graduating from Franklin D. Roosevelt High School. After graduation, she attended Grambling State University. She holds a B.S. degree from Grambling State University, 1975, and a M.S. degree from Louisiana State University, 1986. Loston's professional experience includes Laboratory Supervisor for the City of Shreveport until April 1989. In 1989, she became the Superintendent of Water and Wastewater for the City of Shreveport, where she retired after thirty years of service. She holds many awards and honors including Who is Who Among Americans Scientists.

She is the program coordinator for the science, technology, engineering, and mathematics program funded by the National Science Foundation for Historical Black Colleges and Universities for Undergraduate Program at Southern University, Shreveport. She is also the Coordinator of the LS-LAMP at Southern University, Shreveport. Loston is also a grantwriter and has been awarded many funded projects.

MELVENIA MARTIN, PH.D.

Melvenia M. Martin, Ph.D., is a graduate of Grambling State University. There, she majored in biology with intent of becoming a medical doctor. As a Louisiana Alliance for Minority Participation scholar the LS-LAMP coordinator at the time, Allen Miles, Ph.D., suggested she participate in a summer research program. She applied to several summer programs and was awarded a summer internship at Kansas State University where she began studying "Gravity's effects on soybean growth: a mission to grow plants on NASA's international space station." That summer, Martin's momentum and thought process about science changed. She enjoyed research, and what impact a research scientist could make on the world. After undergraduate graduation, Martin attended Tulane University in New Orleans where she earned her master's degree and doctorate. During her graduate tenure, she was awarded the National Institute of Health's Ruth L Kirschstein National Research Service Award which is a Pre-Doctoral Fellowship used to fund her work of "Environmental Estrogens Regulate HMGA1 and HMGA2 in Benign Uterine Diseases." Before completion of her doctorate, Hurricane Katrina ravished Tulane University causing her to complete her dissertation at Brown University in Providence, Rhode Island before returning to New Orleans, defending, and graduating on time. Upon receiving her degree, Martin accepted a postdoctoral fellowship at the National Institutes of Health/National Cancer Institute in Bethesda, MD. There her work on the underlying mechanism of cancer continued, focusing on DNA repair pathways and replication initiation start sites and how these processes affect cancer's development and growth. After five years at the National Cancer Institute, Martin is as co-coordinator of LS LS-LAMP and an assistant professor of biological sciences where she pursues scientific research, teaches, and serves as a bridge to the doctorate for future scientific researchers.

GEORGE MEAD JR., PH.D.

George F. Mead Jr., Ph.D. earned a bachelor's degree in mathematics from Providence College in Providence, Rhode Island and master's and doctoral degrees in mathematics from the University of Florida. In 1981, Mead came to McNeese as an assistant professor of mathematics and computer science then became department head in 1983.

Prior to arriving at McNeese, he taught mathematics as well as physics at several Florida preparatory schools and a community college. While at McNeese, Mead secured nearly $2 million in federal and state grants to help aid programs for mathematic projects such as Upward Bound, DRIVE, ABLE, in-service training projects for teachers in Calcasieu parish, and mathematics certification and training programs for area teachers.

LEONARD MOORE JR., PH.D.

Leonard Moore Jr., Ph.D., earned dual baccalaureate degrees in chemistry and physics from Grambling State University and a Ph.D. in analytical chemistry from Louisiana State University. As a graduate student, Moore received fellowship support from the Bridge to Doctorate Program Fellowship, Graduate Alliance for Education in Louisiana, and National Organization for the professional advancement of Black Chemists and Chemical Engineers (NOBCChE) Professional Development Award sponsored by Agilent Technologies, Inc. Moore teaches analytical chemistry at GSU and his research interests include advanced studies in the application of polymers for stationary phase separations using electrochromatography.

SYED MUNIRUZZAMAN, PH.D.

Syed Muniruzzaman, Ph.D., is an associate professor of biology at the Xavier University of Louisiana. Prior to joining the faculty at the Xavier University in 2002 he served as an assistant professor of biology at the Jarvis Christian College, Hawkins, Texas. Muniruzzaman earned a doctorate in applied microbiology from Kagawa University, Japan. He also served two stints as a postdoctoral fellow in biochemistry and molecular biology at the University of Arkansas for Medical Sciences, Little Rock, Arkansas and University of Texas Health Science Center, Tyler, Texas. He is the campus coordinator of Louis Stokes Louisiana Alliance for Minority participation program (funded by NSF and Louisiana Board of Regents) at the Xavier University. His research interests are in the area of general microbiology, physiological effect of rare carbohydrates and water quality. He has received funding for his work from National Science Foundation, NASA, LCRC, and Office of Naval Research (sub grant). He is also a certified water quality monitor.

JOE OMOJOLA, PH.D.

Joe Omojola, Ph.D., earned a doctorate in nuclear engineering, and previously served as the dean of the College of Science as well as the chair of the Department of Mathematics and Physics. He is the director of the Enhancement, Enrichment and Excellence in Mathematics and Sciences (E3MaS) grant, which is funded by the National Science Foundation. Omojola is also the campus coordinator for Louis Stokes-Louisiana Alliance for Minority Participation. He is a founding member of the National Alliance for doctoral studies in mathematical sciences. For his outstanding mentoring work, Omojola was awarded the 2006 Presidential Award for Excellence in Science, Mathematics and Engineering Mentoring. He received the award in 2007 at the White House.

SU-SENG PANG, PH.D.

Su-Seng Pang, Ph.D. earned a B.S. degree in mechanical engineering from National Taiwan University, M.S. degree in aerospace engineering and mechanics from University of Minnesota, and Ph.D. degree in mechanical engineering from U.C. Berkeley. Currently, he is the associate vice chancellor for strategic initiatives and the Jack Holmes Distinguished Professor of Mechanical Engineering at Louisiana State University. Pang is a Fellow of three professional societies: American Society of Mechanical Engineers, Society of Plastics Engineers, and American Association for the Advancement of Science. He is a recognized expert in the field of composite materials research. Pang has published more than 200 journal papers/conference proceedings in the areas of composite materials and structures, pressure vessel and piping, and various joining technologies. He has been the Principal Investigator (PI)/Co-PI of 120 projects funded by NSF, NASA, Navy, Army, Air Force, Department of Energy, and various industries. His research/education projects are supporting more than 250 college students per year as well as numerous high school teachers and students. Since 1996, Pang has received 34 U.S. national/regional awards in research and education, including: Presidential Award for Mentoring (at the White House); Tibbetts Award for SBIR Model of Excellence (at the White House); AAAS National Mentor Award; ACAP Distinguished Achievement Award; AACP Outstanding Achievement Award; National Faculty/Administrator Role Model Award; ASME International Board on Minorities and Women Award; Carnegie/CASE Louisiana Professor of the Year; ASEE Nation- al Minorities in Engineering Award; etc. Pang has also received many recognitions from his university, including: LSU Rainmaker Award for Research and Creative Faculty; LSU Making the Difference Award; LSU Award for Faculty Excellence; LSU Distinguished Faculty Award; LSU Alumni Association Faculty Excellence Award; LSU Undergraduate and Graduate Engineering Excellence Mentor Awards; and LSU Engineering Outstanding Faculty Service Award. Currently, Pang is serving as: (i) Board of Director of Applied Polymer Technology Extension Consortium; (ii) External Evaluator for the National Science Foundation (NSF)/HBCU-UP Project at South Carolina State University; (iii) Technical Advisory Committee Member, NASA EPSCoR Program for Louisiana; and (iv) External Evaluator for LSAMP-The Georgia Louis Stokes Alliances for Minority Participation Program. Since 2008, Pang has delivered more than forty invited speeches/ seminars on various education/research topics to numerous universities and organizations in Taiwan, Hong Kong, Macau, China, and United States. He was bestowed an Honorary Doctorate (Doctor of Science honoris causa) from the University of Macau, China in 2006.

ASHOK PURI, PH.D.

Ashok Puri, Ph.D., is a university research professor of physics and campus coordinator of Louis Stokes Louisiana Alliance for Minority participation program, funded by NSF and Louisiana Board of Regents) at the University of New Orleans. Puri is a recipient of Presidential Award for Science, Mathematics and Engineering Mentoring (PASE-MEM, 2005). He is committed to conducting novel forefront research programs with the mission of increasing number of minorities in physics and engineering. Puri has published 70 peer reviewed articles in leading journals including Physical Review Letters, Applied Physics Letters, and Applied Math. Letters, Physics Letters A, Journal of Applied Physics, and Physical Review. He has supervised 18 M.S theses and recently, three graduate students have finished doctoral dissertation in engineering and applied sciences under his supervision. Puri is a fellow of the American Physical Society and has generated about $2 million in grants and contracts. Puri is a naturalized citizen of the United States.

ERIC ROQUE

Eric Roque is the program coordinator for the Louis Stokes Louisiana Alliance for Minority Participation at Tulane University. He is responsible for managing day-to-day programmatic and administrative operations and budgeting and reporting activities of LS-LAMP. Roque is also the budget and administrative coordinator of the University's Center for Engaged Learning and Teaching. Eric has worked at Tulane since 2005 and has been involved with programming associated with increasing participation of underrepresented students in STEM disciplines.

ISIAH M. WARNER, PH.D.

Professor Isiah Warner is an analytical/materials chemist with more than 350 refereed publications and a dozen pending or acquired patents. He has particular expertise in the area of fluorescence spectroscopy, where his research has focused for more than 38 years. Over the past 20 years, he has also maintained a strong research effort in the areas of organized media, separation science, and more recently in the area of ionic liquid chemistry, particularly as applied to solid phase materials for applications in materials science and nanomaterials. Professor Warner's interest in educational research developed early in his academic career. His teaching philosophy has focused on the premise that students can learn science if they are able to function at higher levels of Bloom's ladder and obtain the basic foundation needed for understanding upper-level undergraduate and graduate level courses. This belief has led to funding through numerous educational grants. He also notes that mentoring is a major focus of his role as an academician. As a result of these combined efforts, he has guided (directly and indirectly) hundreds of graduate and undergraduate students to successful careers in STEM. Professor Warner's nationally acclaimed honors give testament to his contributions and commitment to not only his technical field but also to education and students. He received one of the first Presidential Young Investigator Awards from President Ronald Reagan in 1984 and the Presidential Mentoring Award in 1997 from President William Clinton. He has attained LSU's highest professorial rank of Boyd Professor and the American Association for the Advancement of Science (AAAS) Lifetime Mentor award (both in 2000) and was soon after distinguished by the Howard Hughes Medical Institute as one of their inaugural HHMI Professors in 2002. More recently, he has received honor as a Royal Society of Chemistry Fellow (2017), National Academy of Inventors Fellow (2017), SEC Professor of the Year (2016), and induction into the American Academy of Arts and Sciences (2016). He has chaired sixty-five (65) doctoral theses and is currently supervising seven others.

TYRSLAI M. WILLIAMS, PH.D.

Tyrslai Williams is the assistant director for strategic initiatives at Louisiana State University. Williams, a Louisiana native, earned her bachelor's degree, cum laude, in chemistry from Southern University A&M College, Baton Rouge in 2011 and her PhD degree in Organic

Chemistry from Louisiana State University A&M College, Baton Rouge in August of 2017. Williams is also the Director of the eighth cohort of the Louis Stokes Bridge to Doctorate (BD) Initiative. Through this initiative, she instills in her fellows the professional development and interpersonal skills needed to be successful in pursuing a PhD. Her initial appointment as an instructor of organic chemistry laboratory for Louisiana State University allowed her to work with a wide variety of students with very diverse backgrounds, thus, causing an instantaneous ignition of purpose. Williams has since realized her true destiny focuses on providing all students access to higher education in STEM through the conception of intentional holistic programming. As a result, she has been actively involved in pursuing and developing new educational models and programs involving mentoring, broadening participation, informal science learning, interpersonal and holistic development of students at all levels.

ZAKIYA S. WILSON, PH.D.

Zakiya S. Wilson-Kennedy, Ph.D., is an Associate Professor of Research in Chemistry Education and the Assistant Dean for Diversity and Inclusion within the College of Science at Louisiana State University (LSU). Formerly, she held administrative and/or faculty appointments at North Carolina A&T State University, LSU, and the University of Delaware. Dr. Wilson-Kennedy's research investigates the persistence of individuals from all backgrounds in STEM higher education and careers, particularly with regard to faculty and student recruitment, retention and success. With extramural support from NSF, NIH, USDoEd, and philanthropic agencies, she has designed and implemented over 20 education projects, which have employed mentoring models that integrate identity theory and empower-ment theory to create and test development structures that culti-vate self-efficacy and agency, particularly for groups historically underrepresented in STEM. Her work on faculty development uses motivation theory to investigate faculty adoption of and agency with pedagogical reformation and her work on women in higher education focuses on work-life balance policies, practices, and their impact on women of color in the academy. Her educa-tion research has published in peer-reviewed journals, such as the Journal of Science Education and Technology and the Journal of Chemical Education. She served as the principal investigator for the 2014 Presidential Award for Excellence in Science, Math-ematics, and Engineering Mentoring (PAESMEM) organizational recognition for the LSU Office of Strategic Initiatives, and has re-ceived additional national and local honors for her work in broad-ening participation, diversity and STEM education. She is a char-ter member of the Society of STEM Women of Color and the Met-ropolitan Baton Rouge Chapter of the National Coalition of 100 Black Women. She is also a founding contributor to the American Chemical Society (ACS) Women Chemists of Color Initiative. She received her bachelor's degree in chemistry from Jackson State University and her doctorate in computational inorganic chemistry from Louisiana State University

LURIA S. YOUNG, PH.D.

Luria Shaw Young, Ph.D., is the Rosalie Guidry Daste Endowed Professor in Urban Education at Southern University. She earned a bachelor of science in biology from Southern University and A&M College, a master of education and educational specialist certificate in science

education from Louisiana State University, and a doctor of philosophy in educational leadership, research, and counseling from LSU.

Young has a wealth of experience and training in higher education having served in many progressive positions--staff, faculty, and administration. She began her career as an Outreach Generalist with the Southeastern Louisiana University Educational Opportunity Program. After serving in this role for a year, she transferred to Southern University and A&M College as the Louis Stokes Louisiana Alliance for Minority Participation (LS-LAMP) Statewide Evaluations Coordinator. After only one year in this position, Young was promoted to the LS-LAMP Statewide Program Administrator. LS-LAMP is a statewide, coordinated systemic mentoring program aimed at increasing the number and quality of minority students earning baccalaureate and graduate degrees in science, technology, engineering, and mathematics disciplines.

Once Young earned her doctorate, she secured a joint position in the SUBR College of Education, Department of Curriculum and Instruction as an assistant professor and Laser Interferometer Gravitational Wave Observatory (LIGO) Science Education Specialist. Shortly after, Young's knowledge of educator preparation, assessment and student learning outcomes contributed to her being named the National Council for Accreditation of Teacher Education co-coordinator, Board of Examiner for the National Science Teachers Association Pre-service Teacher Education Program, and a Louisiana Board of Examiner.

Young has numerous publications and presentations, and serves as a leader on several federal and state funded initiatives, totaling about $5 million. She is the co-principal investigator of LS-LAMP, the SUBR LIGO Project, and Project Modeling Inquiry Science Education. The latter two projects focus on interfacing formal science education with informal science education using inquiry-based exhibits and "snacks." Young oversees an informal science center, the SUBR LIGO Inquiry Laboratory, in the College of Education. She has been named a Huel D. Perkins Fellow and SUBR Teacher of the Year. Young's research interests include the persistence of students in college, African-American males, and inquiry-based science and mathematics teaching and learning.

LS-LAMP CAMPUSES

DILLARD UNIVERSITY
ABDALLA DARWISH, PH.D.
(504) 816-4840
ADARWISH@DILLARD.EDU

GRAMBLING STATE UNIVERSITY
OLUSEGUN ADEYEMI, PH.D. AND DANNY HUBBARD, PH.D.
(318) 274-6034; (318) 274-8497
ALBURQUERQUE@GRAM.EDU, HUBBARD@GRAM.EDU

LOUISIANA STATE UNIVERSITY
SU-SENG PANG, PH.D.
(225) 578-5892
MEPANG@ME.LSU.EDU

MCNEESE STATE UNIVERSITY
GEORGE MEAD, PH.D.
(337) 475-5785
MEAD@MCNEESE.EDU

NUNEZ COMMUNITY COLLEGE
STEVEN WADDELL
(504) 580-8398
SWADDELL@NUNEZ.EDU

SOUTHERN UNIVERSITY AND A&M COLLEGE
DIOLA BAGAYOKO, PH.D.
(225) 771-2730; (225) 771-4246
BAGAYOKO@AOL.COM

SOUTHERN UNIVERSITY NEW ORLEANS
JOE OMOJOLA, PH.D.
(504) 286-5128; (504) 284-5458
JOMOJOLA@SUNO.EDU

SOUTHERN UNIVERSITY SHREVEPORT
JOSEPHINE P. LOSTON
(318) 670-9329
JLOSTON@SUSLA.EDU

TULANE UNIVERSITY
MICHAEL CUNNINGHAM, PH.D.
(504) 862-3308
MCUNNIN1@TULANE.EDU

UNIVERSITY OF LOUISIANA-LAFAYETTE
VIJAY RAGHAVAN, PH.D. AND BOBBIE DECUIR, PH.D.
(337) 482-6603; (337) 482-6833
RAGHAVAN@LOUISIANA.EDU,
BOBBIE.DECUIR@LOUISIANA.EDU

UNIVERSITY OF NEW ORLEANS
ASHOK PURI, PH.D.
(504) 280-6341
APURI@UNO.EDU

XAVIER UNIVERSITY OF LOUISIANA
MURTY AKUNDI, PH.D.
(504) 520-7647
MAKUNDI@XULA.EDU

www.ingramcontent.com/pod-product-compliance
Lightning Source LLC
Chambersburg PA
CBHW071215090426
42736CB00014B/2827